May the God who is both great and good
make your marriage stronger and your hearts braver.
May He create not only a willingness to die for your marriage,
but also a passion to live for it.

PRAYER

Talking with God

PRAYER

Talking with God

tim+anne evans

PRAYER: Talking with God

Published by REAL LIFE Ministries
PO Box 6800, Colorado Springs, CO 80934

For ordering information visit Amazon.com

DEDICATION

We dedicate *PRAYER*
to every person who longs
for deeper intimacy with God.

CONTENTS

NOTES TO READERS

+ Anne + Tim (we) write from a traditional, Judeo-Christian, orthodox marriage perspective. Our desire is to offer for your consideration marriage views based on forty-three years of marriage, decades of counseling experiences, and a number of Bible passages as we currently understand them. However, we recognize and respect that people have a wide range of beliefs, opinions, and feelings—especially surrounding marriage.

+ Names and details regarding many individuals whose stories are told in this book have been changed to protect their privacy. Editorial liberties have been taken to combine certain people, stories, and circumstances for the purpose of clarity and illustration. In addition, certain portions are reprinted from our **REAL LIFE Marriage**, **TOGETHER, NAKED, SOUL**gasm, or **COMMUNICATION** books.

+ A note to un-married readers: The main focus of this book is for Christian married couples. That said, we believe unmarried readers will also benefit from reading it as they grow in understanding God's creational marriage design, advance in healthy communication skills, live out forgiveness, and embrace godly principles. Always remember God created every person (single and married) in His image. And He gave every man and woman legitimate longings for intimacy and the desire to live life with passion. Remember, the apostle Paul, Mary Magdalene, John the Baptist, and Jesus Christ were all unmarried and led pretty amazing lives. All that is to say, we welcome single readers, and we are grateful for the selfless ways you humbly walk out your love for God and others.

+ Over a decade ago, when we began brainstorming about our **REAL LIFE Marriage** book series, we decided to begin with marriage "in the beginning" and focus on God's creational marriage design. That led to co-authoring **TOGETHER: Reclaiming Co-Leadership in Marriage**.[1] And throughout decades of counseling, we've reached the conclusion that every couple struggles in the area of sexual intimacy. So our next book focused on sexual intimacy—and God is pro-sex! This led to writing **NAKED: Reclaiming Sexual Intimacy in Marriage**.[2] Next, we wrote **SOULgasm**: *Caring for Your Soul and the Soul of Your Marriage*, which focused on the soul-connection between a husband and wife.[3] Our next book, **COMMUNICATION: A Key to Advancing in Intimacy**[4] challenged readers to grow in communicating in healthy ways. This book, **PRAYER: Talking with God** focuses on "advancing" in intimacy with God through prayer. Upcoming books include **FORGIVENESS**, **ABUSE**, **ENGAGED**, and **BEST MARRIAGE NOW**.

+ Whenever we read a book, we like to know a little about the authors. We suspect you may feel the same way. When describing ourselves, first and foremost we say that we are followers of Jesus Christ. Therefore, we purposefully place God at the center of our lives, marriage, family, ministry, relationships, and writing. We have known each other just about all of our lives. We went to kindergarten together, had a crush on each other in middle school, and got married at twenty-one. We are a real-life couple—a retired fire chief and a nurse—who are parents, grandparents, spiritual parents, pastoral counselors, authors, and marriage mentors. Our calling is to be *missionaries to marriage*. We live in Colorado Springs and co-lead REAL LIFE Ministries full time. We've been married forty-three years and by God's grace—and much hard work—we still say, *we love being married*.

Why Should You Invest in Reading this Book?

Countless marriage books and resources are available. While working with couples, we've observed that they aren't looking for another "how-to" book with complicated life applications or the latest "tips-tools-techniques." After all, no guarantees can promise a trouble-free marriage, a passionate prayer life together, or an epic sex life. Instead, our experience has taught us that husbands and wives want to be encouraged, challenged, and spoken to with honesty, relevance, authenticity, and transparency. They want a REAL LIFE model for what it looks like to be in relationship with God in ways that positively impact the intimacy they enjoy with their spouse. Practically speaking, couples are searching for ways they can better understand their true identities, honor covenant, be kind and gracious to each other, and take ownership and responsibility for their individual part in marriage.

+ When observing our culture and listening to the media, one might think that marriage is dying and in need of CPR. From our perspective, we would disagree. While every marriage experiences trouble, we regularly meet husbands and wives who wholeheartedly love God and passionately love their spouses. They have a strong desire for a marriage built on love, functional equality, mutuality, and servanthood. We are also seeing an exciting movement within the Gen-X (Baby Busters), Gen-Y (Millennials), Gen-Z, and emerging Alpha genera-tions[5] as young women and men are revisiting and exploring traditional/orthodox/biblical marriage views.

+ Throughout our REAL LIFE Marriage book series, we remind couples that a Judeo-Christian marriage includes a covenant a man and woman enter into with God and each other. And although "feelings" play a big part in the early attraction phase of relationships, marriage is based on a lifelong—until death parts us—covenant.

+ We regularly remind couples that marriage and covenant are God's ideas—He is pro-mar-riage, pro-intimacy, pro-sex, pro-SOULgasm, and pro-prayer. And after decades of being married and working with many couples, as we pause and reflect on our passion for God's creational marriage design, two things come to our hearts:

#1—EVERY PERSON MATTERS TO GOD—YOU MATTER TO GOD.
#2—GOD'S CREATIONAL MARRIAGE DESIGN MATTERS TO GOD.

+ As we begin our author/reader journey together, we'd like to pray a prayer over every reader:
Lord, please open the hearts of those who invest in reading this book. We pray each reader advances in intimacy with You, better understands their true identity, passion-ately pursues Your creational marriage design, advances in healthy communication, purposefully engages in prayer, humbly walks out forgiveness, and lives in the pres-ent—the now.

LOVE + MARRIAGE ... can you think of any other words that have such life-giving potential?

INTRODUCTION

Book front cover illustrations are important because they provide a first impression of what the authors are writing about. We invest a lot of time, energy, and resources determining the illustration for each of our books. For example, our *TOGETHER Reclaiming Co-Leadership in Marriage* front cover has a custom designed triple-traffic-light illustration. Our *NAKED Reclaiming Sexual Intimacy in Marriage* front cover illustration is a man and women standing side-by-side in a Garden of Eden-like setting. For our *SOULGASM Caring for Your Soul and the Soul of Your Marriage* book Anne designed an exclamation point! And *COMMUNICATION A Key to Advancing in Intimacy* has dialogue blips.

Regarding prayer, of course, a person can pray about *anything—anywhere—anytime*. And throughout this book we will offer readers dozens of suggestions for developing a vibrant and creative prayer life. On the other hand, our experience is, in addition to praying *wherever* and *whenever* a person wants, it can be valuable to have a *specific place* to regularly meet and commune with God. A place that is familiar, has meaning and history, and brings comfort and joy to the person praying.   .

For example, early in our marriage when we lived in a small ranch home in the Chicago suburbs, Anne had a desk in our bedroom that became her special place to pray. She created artwork and placed favorite Bible texts and important quotes that were meaningful to her on the wall above her desk. At that time, Tim's special place to pray indoors was in the living room where he knelt and prayed in front of a large wing-back chair. And often, Tim would begin his day with a jog, and he'd finish at a park bench near our home where he prayed.

When we moved to Michigan, Anne selected a large closet that she creatively filled with things she enjoyed and which encouraged her to pray. Tim found another prayer bench near our home. It was at *Tunnel Park* and sat on a bluff overlooking Lake Michigan. Almost every morning he would finish his jog praying at that bench. On weekends, and often after supper, we would both walk to that bench, take in the majesty of the lake—and pray together.

From Michigan we moved to Pasadena, California, and we found a bench near our apartment that we regularly prayed at. We currently live in Colorado Springs, and we've found a number of natural rock benches on our hikes in *Red Rock Canyon* where we stop and pray. For this book, *PRAYER Talking with God*, we chose for the book front cover illustration a simple drawing of a bench that represents many of our prayer benches.

We pray that after reading this book *you* will find special places to pray. This might be a desk, a chair, your kitchen table, a closet—or a bench. As we look back over forty-three years of marriage, and counseling/mentoring countless couples, our experience is husbands and wives who make praying together a high life priority will advance in intimacy—and in spirit + soul + body oneness.

+ + +

Change can be difficult. It's easy to read a book and feel intrigued or challenged by what you read. But you may still go on with your life, avoiding any necessary steps to make positive changes based on what you read. Whether you are going through this book with your spouse or in a REAL LIFE marriage community group, we challenge you to strategically take next steps toward advancing in intimacy with God, your spouse, and others.

We have designed every chapter to engage couples on a variety of levels. For those going through the book as a group, as you begin, you may want to invest more than one meeting on a certain chapter. The goal is not to finish this book, but to learn together and grow in community. Therefore, you have total freedom to customize each chapter to best suit your needs, desires, and schedules. At the end of every chapter there are questions, challenges, and applications, including the following questions:

REAL LIFE Questions

Each question invites you to dig into the content on a deeper level. Our hope is you will take time to explore the truths that the questions are prompting. Remember, the goal is not to *retreat* from answering difficult questions, but to *advance* in intimacy with God and your spouse. And to grow in community with those in your community group.

Note on confidentiality: It's important to establish and maintain healthy boundaries in marriage. This includes respecting each other's privacy and honoring each other's stories. That is why it is important to be in agreement—in other words, both husband and wife have green lights (for an explanation of the Traffic Light Principle, see Appendix A)—before sharing about your marriage in a group. We encourage you to focus on telling your own story, rather than your spouse's or someone else's story.

REAL LIFE Couples Application

This section invites couples to process questions and challenges together. The Bible says, "Those who marry will face many troubles..." (1 Corinthians 7:28 NIV). We've been married over four decades, and we have experienced marital troubles. Truth be told, we continue to experience troubles. The key to dealing with troubles is how you respond to them, individually and as a couple.

Experience has taught us that when a husband and wife take ownership and responsibility for their part in marriage by including God (2 Corinthians 10:5), asking for wisdom (James 1:5), and growing up (1 Corinthians 13:11), *obstacles* can become *opportunities*. And these opportunities often become pathways to advancing in intimacy and in spirit + soul + body oneness.

+ **Listening to God + I.O.T.L.**—see Appendix B: Listening to God and Appendix C: Inquire of the Lord (**I.O.T.L.**). At the end of each chapter, we challenge you to engage with God by using the acronym **I.O.T.L.** This refers to the Old Testament phrase "inquire of the Lord." Inviting God into your process and practicing the discipline of listening are intimacy-advancing exercises.

If you are a follower of Jesus Christ, the Holy Spirit dwells in you (Romans 8:9). The Bible instructs followers of Christ, saying, "See to it that you do not refuse Him who is speaking…" (Hebrews 12:25). This involves inviting your good Father into your process. Each chapter's questions and applications will encourage you to ask for wisdom (James 1:5) as you access the One who longs to be included in every area of your life. Remember, this is not a religious exercise; it involves a person relating to God. Imagine a child saying to a good mommy or daddy, "I trust you. Please give me wisdom and help me make good decisions."

A Few Thoughts

In our own marriage, and as we've worked with couples, we have found that living out the miracle and mystery of two becoming one (Genesis 2:24) and fully celebrating what it means to be naked without shame (Genesis 2:25) does not occur magically. Rather, it involves an intentional investment of time, energy, and resources. From personal experience, we've seen that trusting God and taking risks are pathways to advancing in intimacy with God and each other, all of which pay rich dividends that can be passed on for generations.

We challenge you to make this book study a priority. If you are going through this book with others, take some time and review your schedules. Agree on specific dates and times when you will meet. Writing this down will encourage accountability. We agree to meet on:

_____

_____

Also, write down contact information for each member (phone numbers, email addresses, home addresses, etc.). You may want to add anniversary dates, birthdays, and any children's names and ages.

_____

_____

We are excited for you to take this journey. As you go forward in hope, freedom, and joy, know that we are praying for you, your spouse, and every community group that is going through this book.

As you begin this book, take an overview of your marriage.

Date: _____

On a continuum from 1 to 10:

[1=Our marriage is very disconnected to 10=Our marriage couldn't be better]

How would you rate your marriage in this current season? _____

How do you think your spouse would rate your marriage in this current season? _____

As you consider your responses, make two observations related to your marriage in this current season. [Note: you will not be asked to share this.]

_____

_____

Concerning prayer, how would you rate your prayer life with your spouse? _____

How do you think your spouse would rate their prayer life with you? _____

As you consider your responses, make two observations specifically related to your prayer life. [Note: you will not be asked to share this.]

_____

_____

Throughout our REAL LIFE Marriage book series, we encourage couples to always have dreams for their marriage. And when you dream—dream BIG! Write down two marriage dreams you have in this season of your marriage.

_____

_____

We are asking for God's favor, protection, and blessings as you advance in intimacy with God, your spouse, and others. We bless you and are prayerfully cheering you on.

With love,

anne+tim evans

www.TimPlusAnne.com

PREFACE

LIFE IS LIVED IN A STORY

anne

I grew up in a praying family. When my parents took us to church, I watched them kneel down, fold their hands, and close their eyes to pray. Occasionally I would hear them say to someone, "We're praying for you." When we gathered together for a family meal, my dad would lead us in praying; "Bless us, oh Lord, and these Thy gifts, which we are about to receive from Thy bounty, through Christ our Lord. Amen."

As children we prayed, *The Lord's Prayer*. For years I repeated the exact same words to God every night, "Our Father who art in heaven, hallowed be thy name. Thy kingdom come; Thy will be done on earth as it is in heaven..." Even as a child I must have had a desire for a more personal connection with God, because at the end of the Lord's Prayer I always added a personal message. It went like this, "God bless Mom, Dad, Patty, John, Colleen, Skokie Grandma, Skokie Papa, big Gram and big Papa. God bless all my friends and relatives, make me good and keep me healthy. Amen."

As a child, my bedtime request for blessings was the closest I ever got to a personal conversation with God. As I was growing up my prayers remained virtually the same. I viewed God as an omniscient, all powerful Creator rather than as a loving Father who longed to be in relationship with me.

Looking back, it never occurred to me to ask my parents *why* they prayed, *what* they prayed, or *if* God ever answered their prayers. As a child, none of those questions seemed to matter. What made the deepest impression on me was the simple knowledge *that* my parents prayed. My dad and mom modeled a consistent prayer life that provided the foundation for how I related to God. That foundation taught me that prayer was important; it was a bridge that enabled me to connect to God.

✛ ✛ ✛

Life Is Lived in a Story

tim

As I was growing up, my mom frequently reminded her daughter and four sons that prayer was important. In addition to meal times, we were encouraged to pray for our family, friends, and those in need. I remember mom reminding us to "say a special prayer" for someone who was sick, was having surgery, or had lost a loved one. And as long as we lived at home, we were required to go to church, where mom instructed us to pray that we'd *have a good week.*

Our family of seven grew up in a small three-bedroom ranch home, and my three brothers and I shared a bedroom. When we were young kids, mom often reminded us to end our day by saying a prayer. I recall mine being more like a declaration. Before my head hit the pillow, I'd say to the Lord and to our family—*good night + prayers + thanks for everything!* Apparently, I thought if I simply used the word "prayers" it would cover a multitude of requests. And throughout my years growing up, if I didn't fall asleep right away, I remember the familiar sound of my mom's prayer rosary beads hitting the wooden floor as she fell asleep.

Once I got my driver's license, I would come home late on weekends. As I turned the corner and drove down our short dead-end street, I knew my mom was waiting up for me—praying. I could see the glow from her cigarette through the bay window in our living room. There she would sit in a chair waiting for all of us to get home. As I entered the house, I'd often whisper, *"Mom, what are you doing staying up so late?"*

She'd smile and say, "I'm praying that everyone gets home safely before I go to bed."

I am thankful my mom was a woman who prayed. And I don't think I will ever fully understand, this side of heaven, the power and protection my mom's prayers provided me and our family. I know her prayers were sincere, I believe God heard them, and I'm certain they protected us. Mom's faith and consistent prayer life left a deep impression on me, and her example encouraged me to devote myself to prayer.[1]

How a person views God and prayer can often be traced back to what they saw modeled, and what they experienced—both positively and negatively—in their family of origin. One thing for certain is every relationship takes time, even a relationship with God. And as intimacy and trust grow, often a person discovers they are inviting God into more and more areas in their life as they talk—and listen to God.

How about you? As you review your family of origin, how does your story relate to prayer? As a married couple, we have found that a vibrant prayer life is an important key to advancing in intimacy with God—and each other. And being married over four decades, as we review our marriage, when we have purposefully made prayer a high priority, in addition to advancing in intimacy, it has resulted in advancing in seeing ourselves, each other, and others in ways that our good Father does. Prayer connects to growing in, and living out, our true identity—as God's *beloved* daughter and son.

✚ ✚ ✚

Larger Story vs. Smaller Story

Throughout our REAL LIFE marriage book series, we say, *life is lived in a story*. We believe a person can choose to live in one of two stories, the Larger Story or the smaller story. The way to determine which story you are living in is to ask a simple question, *who is the main character in my story?* If the main character in your story is *you*—you are living in the smaller story. And if the main character in your story is *God*—you are living the Larger Story.[2]

As you process through each chapter, we will invite you to step into the Larger Story by practicing the presence of God through prayer. In the Larger Story, where God is the main character, prayer can help you advance in intimacy with Him, your spouse, and others.

REAL LIFE Questions

1. *Life is lived in a story*. As you review *your* family of origin story, what observations can you make.

How did your family view God? Prayer?

_____

_____

How did that model influence *your* view of God and prayer?

_____

_____

As you review *your spouse's* family of origin story, what observations can you make.
How do you think your spouse's family viewed God? Prayer?

_____

_____

How did that model influence *their* view of God and prayer?

_____

_____

2. A person can live in one of two stories, the Larger Story or the smaller story. If the main character in your story is *you*—you are living in the smaller story. And if the main character in your story is *God*—you are living the Larger Story.

Give an example of a time when you chose to live in the *Larger Story*.

_____

_____

Give an example of a time when you chose to live in the *smaller story*.

_____

_____

3. Throughout our authors/reader journey together we are going to encourage you to include God in your daily life and decisions. Be intentional to engage Him through prayer by simply talking to Him.

Are you ready to take steps to advance in intimacy with God?   Yes_____ No_____
Briefly describe what steps you are ready to take.

_____

_____

REAL LIFE Couples Application

The Bible says, "Where there is no *vision*, the people perish."[3]
Pause for a moment and envision including God in more areas in your life and decision-making process. Briefly describe how that decision could positively impact *you*.

_____

_____

Briefly describe how the choice to include God in more areas of your life and decision-making process could positively impact *your marriage*.

_____

_____

Set aside time to share with your spouse how you responded to the section above.

_____

_____

Listening to God—I.O.T.L. (*Inquire of the Lord*).

Inviting God into your day by including Him, even in the little things, is one way to build intimacy with Him. Hebrews 12:25 says, "See to it that you do not refuse Him who is speaking." In other words, God *is* speaking, but are you taking the time to listen? At the end of each chapter, we include a *Listening to God* section. This provides an opportunity to *Inquire of the Lord* (I.O.T.L.) and ask the following questions:

+ *Lord, is there anything You want to highlight for me in this section?*

_____

+ *Is there a specific step You want me to take?*

_____

+ *Is there anything You would like me to share with my spouse?*

_____

+ *Journal anything you sense the Lord may be saying to you.*

_____

_____

CHAPTER 1

THE MYSTERY OF PRAYER

In a book titled *Prayer*, Richard Foster describes the mystery that happens every time a person prays. He says coming to prayer is like coming home.

> Nothing feels more right, more like what we are created to be and to do. Yet at the same time we are confronted with great mysteries. Who hasn't struggled with the puzzle of unanswered prayer? Who hasn't wondered how a finite person can commune with an infinite Creator of the universe? Who hasn't questioned whether prayer isn't merely psychological manipulation after all? We do our best, of course, to answer these knotty questions but when all is said and done, there is a sense in which these mysteries remain unanswerable.... At such times we must learn to be comfortable with the mystery.[1]

The Miracle and Mystery of Prayer

Just as the marriage relationship, in which a husband and wife become one,[2] is both a miracle and a mystery, so is prayer. The miracle is being able to communicate with the great I AM, the Creator of everything. The mystery is God's desire to relate back to us in ways that draw a person into deeper intimacy with Him.

The Bible says, "If any of you lacks wisdom, let him ask of God, who gives to all generously and without reproach, and it will be given to him."[3] This verse presupposes relationship with God. It encourages talking to Him: you ask, and listen. And when it comes to listening to God, the Bible says, "Do not refuse Him who is speaking." This verse presupposes God is speaking and gives a stern warning to listen—to not refuse Him. The Scriptures encourage you to engage in ongoing communication with your good Father. Engaging in prayer by simply talking to God is an invitation to draw closer to Him; it can become an opportunity to advance in intimacy.

Similarly, the covenant of marriage can be described as ongoing dialogue between a husband and wife. This includes intentionally creating space to talk—and listen—to each other. The marriage relationship also invites a couple to advance in intimacy with God through prayer. Just as a husband and wife make it a priority to communicate with one another—God also invites them to participate in an ongoing dialogue with Him.

Prayer is the starting place. It's how a person begins to relate to God. Praying—simply talking to God—is how a person can know they are intimately known and unconditionally loved by a good Father. Prayer is a way to connect with God. It's a vehicle to know Him and to be known by Him. Prayer is a two-way relationship—not a one-person monologue. It's a bridge that connects a *created* (child) to the *Creator* (God). Prayer is a form of surrender and a way to release control as you place your trust in the One who is trustworthy.

People pray for many reasons. Some pray out of reverence for God. Some simply are making their requests known to God.[5] Some are looking for direction or answers. And others pray because they know there is no better place to go than to God.

Regardless of *why* a person prays, we believe it is important *that* a person prays. Whether you are thanking God, asking for strength, seeking wisdom,[6] or trying to better understand things from God's perspective, prayer is connection with God. It is an invitation to include God in your life—and marriage. It reflects a desire to know Him and to be known by Him.

In marriage, discovering how to merge your individual styles of prayer can sometimes present a challenge. We've learned that being a *good listener* is a vital part of a shared prayer life. But listening is a learned skill that takes practice, and for most people, listening well does not come naturally. In our experience, slowing down and purposefully investing in becoming a better listener not only helps your prayer life with God, but it will also positively impact intimacy in your marriage and other relationships in your life.

Couples who regularly pray together tell us that once they found a way to pray together that worked for them, it bonded them to God and each other in ways they couldn't have imagined. One couple told us, "When we are praying, it's like we become a dynamic *team* working together." Prayer is a way for couples to declare *dependence* on God and *interdependence* with each other. It's a way of saying, "Father, we can't do this—we don't want to do this—without You." Prayer uniquely positions a couple to *advance* in spirit + soul + body oneness.

Some people lean toward a more formal, traditional, or liturgical style. While others like their conversations with God to be organic and free-flowing. When it comes to prayer and being in relationship with someone you love, there is no right or wrong style of sharing your heart. After all,

> Peter knelt, Jeremiah stood, Nehemiah sat down, Abraham prostrated himself, and Elijah put his face between his knees. In Jesus' day most Jews stood, lifting their open eyes to heaven. The Virgin Mary prayed in poetry; Paul interspersed his prayers with singing.[7]

In marriage, when a husband and wife *reflect* and *reveal* the heart of Jesus to each other, this can be a form of prayer. When a couple celebrates sexual intimacy—and enjoy God's two-be-come-one[8] and naked-without-shame[9] design for marriage, it can become a form of prayer. When a couple is listening to worship music, or biking or hiking together, these can be forms of prayer. Prayer can include a tender touch or an encouraging look that conveys God's love, kindness, and care to a spouse.

Prayer is turning your internal dialogue toward the One who is speaking[10]—and listening.[11] God has the power to intervene, to transform a heart, to change a circumstance, or to comfort someone who is hurting. Prayer can be an intention of the heart that doesn't require specific words. Prayer can be an attitude of praise, worship, or thanksgiving. Prayer can be a response to a person who is lost, grieving, or in the midst of experiencing joy. Connecting with your Creator—and *together* with your spouse—rejuvenates you and leads to advancing in intimacy.

Teach Us to Pray

When the disciples asked Jesus, "Teach us to pray...,"[12] He didn't respond by explaining the mysteries of a complicated spiritual discipline that was reserved for an elite few. Instead of teaching tools, tips, and techniques about prayer, Jesus instructed His disciples to begin with God, saying, "When you pray, say: "'*Father....*"[13] As an aside, it's interesting that Jesus' disciples did not say, "Teach us *how to pray.*" They said to Jesus, "Teach us *to pray.*"

Surely the suggestion to approach God as *Father* took the disciples by surprise. After all, *father* is a name that relates to an earthly *relationship*. The very thought of God as a *father* suggests that intimacy is available through relationship with Him. We suspect that Jesus knew that if His disciples were going to be intimately connected to God, they would need to understand that God is like a good father who longs to be in relationship with his *beloved* children. And we have reached the conclusion that a person's understanding of *who God is* directly relates to their ability to live out their true identity as a *beloved* son or daughter of a good God.

People view God in all sorts of ways. For some, He is a stern judge, powerful Creator, distant, disinterested, or a task master. As a person's relationship with God continues to mature, hopefully, they come to know Him as their good Father. Someone they long to invite into every moment of their day. This includes the routine *ordinary* moments, as well as *extraordinary* moments.[14] In our experience, an ongoing relationship with God is the foundation of our prayer lives as we intentionally invite Him into our hearts, lives, marriage, and ministry.

The disciples' lesson on prayer continued. Jesus said to them, "When you pray, say: "'...hallowed be Your name....'"[15] In other words, the Father that Jesus is talking about is nothing like any human father you have ever known. God the Father is unique, set apart, and holy.[16]

The Bible doesn't tell us *why* the disciples asked Jesus to teach them to pray. But we can speculate. People are curious about the mysteries surrounding prayer for a variety of reasons. Perhaps the disciples longed for the same kind of intimate relationship that Jesus shared with His Father. Maybe they had questions or doubts that needed answers. Maybe they were filled with gratitude and wanted to know how to express their natural human emotions to a supernatural God.

We don't know for sure, but we do know this—every human being is created in the image of God.[17] God is a Triune God—Father + Jesus + Holy Spirit. The Bible says, "The grace of the Lord *Jesus Christ*, and the love of *God*, and the fellowship of the *Holy Spirit*, be with you all."[18] And just like the Triune God interrelates in community as one, so too, as God's image-bearers, every man and woman is created with a longing to live in community, to experience intimacy, to connect with God and others, and in marriage to experience God's amazing *two-become-one* design.[19] In addition to praying to God, as a person invites God into every moment in their lives, an important next step is *listening* for Him to respond. And as we've said, the Bible says, "Do not refuse Him who is speaking."[20]

Life Is Lived in a Story

tim

We read in the Scriptures how Jesus continued to point His disciples to the Father. He taught those closest to Him to pray—to simply talk to God—to address Him as Father. As young parents, Anne and I also had a desire for our children to enjoy relationship with God. We read in the Old Testament that after Moses was given the Ten Commandments, God directed him to teach Israel to observe His commands and pass them onto their children so that they would enjoy life and increase in the land that was flowing with milk and honey. Moses addressed the generational impact of living in relationship with God. He said to all of Israel,

> *You shall love the Lord your God with all your heart and with all your soul and with all your might. These words, which I am commanding you today, shall be on your heart. You shall teach them diligently to your sons and shall talk of them when you sit in your house and when you walk by the way and when you lie down and when you rise up. You shall bind them as a sign on your hand and they shall be as frontals on your forehead. You shall write them on the doorposts of your house and on your gates.*[21]

One of the strongest lessons parents can give their children on prayer is simply modeling their own personal relationship with God to them. Proverbs 20:7 challenges us to walk in integrity so our lives become the lesson we teach our children.

When our children were younger and began to attend Sunday school, they heard a familiar phrase challenging them to, "Accept Jesus into their hearts." While that decision is an important one, it was never meant to be a single event in a person's life that is celebrated, but often soon forgotten. Instead, it represents a starting place. Accepting Jesus is a decision a person makes to place God as the main character in their life—and story. Hopefully, as they continue to advance in intimacy with God, prayer becomes a natural part their journey.

Every relationship will have ups and downs—including a person's relationship with God. There will be times when a person's heart is deeply connected to their decision to follow God. And at other times, the decision to love feels more like a commitment. One thing for sure is that God will never force His way into a person's heart, life, or marriage. Instead, He gives every person the freedom to choose Him. He is a God defined by intimate relationship, not a God of religion and rules. For those who commit to journeying with Him through life, learning to pray and talk with Him becomes a growing part of that relationship.

Every relationship has a starting point. As parents, it has been such a joy to watch our children grow in their relationships and prayer lives. And as grandparents, it is difficult to describe seeing our children mentoring our grandchildren in prayer and the importance of being in relationship with God.

Life Is Lived in a Story

anne

Over the years, I recall conversations with my daughters that were focused on their children's bedtime routines. As I've watched my children raising their own children, I smile when their experiences sound familiar to my own memories of being a young parent. For example, the struggle to get kids to bed at night seems to be one of those things that hasn't changed with the passing of time.

When I was a young parent, I decided that children must have some sort of built-in sensor when the sun goes down. It seemed that whenever it was time for my kids to go to bed, they suddenly have a million *really important* things they want to tell me. While the list seemed endless, it often included a familiar list of revelations and requests. Such as, "I'm *not tired*. I'm thirsty. I have to go to the bathroom. This blanket is itchy. I have a cramp in my leg. My tummy feels funny when I lay down. And a long list of other things that seemed to make it impossible for them to fall asleep. No matter how much time Tim and I set aside to listen, there seemed to always be just *one more thing* they forgot to tell us...

When Tim and I were growing up, our parents modeled a more traditional and liturgical style of prayer. However, as we grew into adulthood, our relationship with God began to change. And that change impacted our prayer life. As our trust in Him grew stronger, our prayers became less traditional and more conversational.

When our children became parents, I remember conversations with my daughter about similar struggles at bedtime. I encouraged her to try new things with her kids before bedtime. For example, instead of leading them in a traditional bedtime prayer, I encouraged her to practice creating some space for them to be still, to wait, and to listen to God.

Sometime later, my daughter shared what happened. One night after her kids brushed their teeth, went potty, had a sip of water, and were all tucked in, my daughter asked them if they wanted to try something new. Of course, their response was an enthusiastic, *yes!* My daughter quietly invited them, "Close your eyes, and think about God. Ask Him if there is anything He wants to say before you go to sleep." She continued leading them by making suggestions. At one point she said, "There might be something you want to ask God. Or something you want to give Him so you can fall asleep. It might be something you have been carrying in your heart all day. You can hand him any worries or unfinished stories. And you can ask Him to hold those things for you—so you can get a good night's sleep." The room became quiet as they considered her suggestions.

As a parent, you get a glimpse of what it means to *become like children*.[22] I could just picture their little eyes closed tightly as they listened. Their response to the challenge modeled childlike faith in a good Father God. Of course, a parent can never predict a child's requests or response, but seeing them inviting God into their lives and stories opens up all kinds of conversations. All that is to say, when you leave space for God, it often opens the door to connection, relationship, experiencing community, and advancing in intimacy.

+ + +

A person who prays is someone, young or old, who is comfortable talking to God. They also seem to know when to talk and when to listen. Whether they are praying in private, public, a small group setting, or large gathering, their conversation with God seems to be as natural for them as breathing. And when a person who has a vibrant prayer life says, "I'll pray for you"—they mean it. They have experienced and believe in the power of prayer. Often for them, including God is their first thought.

Throughout our married life, God has blessed us with people who have been a model to us of what it means to pray. They are people who have faithfully prayed for our marriage, family, and ministry. We consider these women and men to be prayer mentors. And as we observed their relationship with God, it provided an invitation to us, and to those around them, to "taste and see that the Lord is good."[23] Regarding prayer, their never-ending, easy-flowing conversations with God encouraged us to include God throughout our everyday lives, in both ordinary and extraordinary moments—and to pray.

One example, we met Dick Swetman shortly after we were married. He and his wife Alice became our first small-group leaders. Throughout our kid's growing up years, Dick became like a spiritual father. For decades he mentored us in prayer, and he also prayed every day on his knees for each member of our family until he passed away in his mid-eighties. As our children continued to grow up, got married, and had children of their own, he added each new family member to his prayer list. We truly believe his prayers protected our marriage and family in immeasurable ways.

REAL LIFE Questions

1. Briefly describe from your own life an example of the miracle of prayer.

_____

_____

2. Briefly describe from your own life an example of the mystery of prayer.

_____

_____

3. In what specific ways do the following statements on prayer relate to your own life?

Prayer is a bridge that connects a created (child) to the Creator (God).

_____

_____

Prayer is a form of surrender and a way to release control as you place your trust in the One who is trustworthy.

_____

_____

4. Do you have any prayer mentors in your life? If so, write down their names and thank God for them.

_____

_____

If you do not have any prayer mentors in your life, ask God to give you at least one. Journal your request to God below:

_____

_____

5. If you are willing to become a prayer mentor, list the names of people you would like to pray for and mentor. Then contact them and explain what you are thinking related to prayer.

_____

_____

REAL LIFE Couples Application

In what ways could surrendering and releasing control benefit your marriage and prayer life as a couple?

_____

_____

_____

_____

Schedule a time/date and together review your answers to the above questions.

_____

_____

Listening to God—I.O.T.L. (*Inquire of the Lord*)

Inviting God into your day by including Him, even in the little things, is one way to build intimacy with Him. Hebrews 12:25 says, "See to it that you do not refuse Him who is speaking." In other words, God *is* speaking, but are you taking the time to listen? At the end of each chapter, we include a *Listening to God* section. This provides an opportunity to *Inquire of the Lord* (I.O.T.L.) and ask the following questions:

+ *Lord, is there anything You want to highlight for me in this section?*

_____

_____

+ *Is there a specific step You want me to take?*

_____

_____

+ *Is there anything You would like me to share with my spouse?*

_____

_____

+ Journal anything you sense the Lord may be saying to you.

_____

_____

CHAPTER 2

LISTENING TO GOD

Communication is an important part of every relationship.[1] Part of being a good communicator includes being able to effectively convey what's on your mind and in your heart. However, *speaking* is only one part of good communication. Another part that is equally important is being a *good listener*. In fact, good listening skills are crucial to advancing in intimacy with God, a spouse, and others. Imagine the negative impact to a relationship if one person did all the talking and was not a very good listener.

Mother Theresa said, "God speaks in the silence of the heart. Listening is the beginning of prayer."[2] The Bible emphasizes the importance of *inquiring of the* Lord (**I.O.T.L.**) and listening to God. It says, "See to it that you do not refuse Him who is speaking."[3] As pastoral counselors, we have observed that most people struggle with being a good listener. Often, they admit to placing a greater focus on talking and being heard than on listening to what is being said or what is *not* being said. This results in poor communication, which is an intimacy-blocker with a spouse, others, and God. Concerning prayer, it's easy to get so focused on what you want to *say* to God that you neglect the importance of simply *listening*. This Hebrews passage is a reminder that *God is speaking*, and it's up to you to take the time to listen.

One way for a person to listen to the "one who *is speaking*"[4] is to quiet their heart and mind. Psalms 46:10 (NIV) says, "Be still, and know that I am God." The act of *being still* is a decision, a discipline, and a practice. It's in the sacredness in silence where a person may experience a new thought or an impression that might be from our good Father. Listening prayer often softens a person's heart and creates space for God to speak. And when a person's heart is sensitive to God, whatever He may be inviting them to do is much more important than anything they may have planned.

The Bible is filled with stories of God speaking to people. Beginning in Genesis, He spoke to Adam and Eve in the garden. God spoke to Noah with instructions regarding the ark. God spoke to Moses from a burning bush. The apostle Paul heard the voice of God on the road to Damascus. And the risen Christ spoke to Mary at the tomb shortly after He was resurrected. So *yes*, God speaks.

If you are asking, "Does God *still* speak—and can He speak to me audibly?" Our answer again is *yes*. That said, we understand there are people whose theology restricts God from speaking, because they believe everything He wanted to say is in the Bible. Personally, it concerns us when *created* humans attempt to determine what the *creator* God can—and cannot—do or say.

We believe God still speaks and communicates to people in all sorts of different ways. For example, we have heard God speak through His Word. Second Timothy 3:16 (NIV) says, "All Scripture is God-breathed." We have also heard God speak during prayer. That said, we have rarely heard Him speak in audible words. Instead, we hear what He is saying in our hearts. In fact, knowing God hears our prayers and communicates with us is a big motivation for us to pray. In addition, God has spoken to us through other people. Their audible voice echoes the voice of our Father, aligns with the principles of Scripture, and strengthens, encourages, comforts, challenges, cautions, and convicts us.

God often speaks through circumstances and experiences in our lives. He regularly speaks to us through nature and creation.[5] We've experienced God speaking every time a child or grandchild is born, as well as when someone dies. He speaks through music, worship, song writers, lyricists, poets,[6] and musicians. These experiences rekindle our passion, comfort our pain, calm our fears, and restore our hope.

Of course, God speaks through the Holy Spirit. The voice of the Great Counselor and En-courager has been described as a still, soft voice.[7] As our Guide, the Holy Spirit directs us, strengthens us, and encourages us to live in humility, with integrity, and to pursue truth. And if we get off track, we hear God's voice through conviction in our hearts.

The Bible says, "For the eyes of the Lord range throughout the earth to *strengthen* those whose *hearts* are *fully committed to Him.*"[8] Being strong in the Lord involves being sensitive to the Spirit of God. This includes inviting God to *strengthen* you, developing a *heart* that is *fully committed to Him*, focusing on listening well, releasing control—and being willing to respond with prayer.

Similarly, in marriage, husbands and wives who are committed to each other, and willing to listen and pray, can choose to be sensitive to the Spirit of God. These kinds of intentional choices help couples to *advance* in intimacy with God—and each other.

Life Is Lived in a Story

tim

My experience is at times God speaks by placing a *burden* on a person's heart. When I use the term *burden*, I am referring to feeling the shared weight or responsibility for something God values. I may feel the weight of injustice, pain, or struggle—and respond with prayer. I believe God is speaking when He brings to mind a person, situation, or new thought—and I can choose to respond with prayer.

For example, as I was reviewing this chapter before sending the manuscript to our editor, out of nowhere, a good friend of mine came to my heart. I know my friend is currently living in Los Angeles trying to get his book made into a movie. And I know a few of the many obstacles he has faced. When my friend came to my mind, I stopped reading the manuscript and prayed for him. I asked God to encourage him, open up divine appointments, bless him, provide for and protect him, and give him favor. After I prayed, I sent him a quick text to let him know I was thinking about—and praying for him. And then I returned to proofreading this chapter.

+ + +

Four Voices

In a world filled with countless choices and many voices, it's easy to get overwhelmed. Therefore, it's important for a person to be able to listen so they can identify who is speaking. It's vital to be able to differentiate between truth, deception, manipulation, and lies. And this involves growing in your ability to distinguish between the many voices screaming for your attention.

We believe there are four voices a person can listen to. The way to determine which voice you are hearing is to simply ask yourself this question: *Who am I listening to?*

     1- my *own* voice?

     2- the voice of *others?*

     3- the *enemy's* voice?

     4- *God's* voice?

Whenever a person is talking, they are obviously able to hear and discern *their own* voice. The same is true when *others* are speaking. When we refer to *hearing God's voice*, we are not referring to the audible voice of God. Instead, we encourage you to pay attention to the heart of what you sense He may be saying. The heart of God is to speak to you with words that are strengthening, encouraging, and comforting. His words are kind and life-giving. And while they may be convicting, they are never shaming.

However, the voice of the enemy is the opposite. His words are always negative, shaming, blaming, and condemning. The voice of the enemy aims to attack a person's identity as he uses lies and false identity statements that are directly opposed to the truth of who God says we are—His *beloved* daughters and sons.

Before moving on, it's important to note that often *my* voice, or the voice of *others*, can mimic the voice of *God*—or the *enemy*. Words *have power*, they can be encouraging and life-giving or discouraging, toxic, and life-sucking. That's why it is important to pay close attention to the words you are hearing and the voices you are listening to.

+ + +

Becoming a Good Listener

Listening to God is one of the most important things you can do as a son/daughter of a good Father. The Bible says, "See to it that you do not refuse Him who is speaking."[9] As your relationship with God grows, your confidence in Him will increase. And this will enable you to recognize who you are listening to.

As a person matures, an important part of life includes making godly decisions. James 1:5 (NLT) says, "If you need wisdom, ask our generous God, and he will give it to you. He will not rebuke you for asking." We have put together a list of twelve questions that are also in Appendix B. We encourage you to consider these questions in your decision-making process. Following are a number of principals found in God's Word.

1. Have you prayed about what you are considering? [Philippians 4:6; 2 Corinthians 10:5]
2. Is what you are considering consistent with the principles in the Bible? [1 Corinthians 2:25; James 1:5 NIV]
3. Is what you are considering affirmed by other godly people? [Proverbs 11:14]
4. Will what you are considering bring glory to God? [Colossians 3:17]
5. Will what you are considering positively impact God's kingdom? [Matthew 6:33]
6. How does what you are considering relate to God's will for your life? [1 Thessalonians 5:16–18]
7. Do you have peace about what you are considering? [Philippians 4:7 ESV]
8. Do you have unity with your spouse [both have green lights]? [Genesis 1–2]
9. Will what you are considering cost you something? [Luke 18:29–30]
10. Does what you are considering agree with your life calling and mission? [Ephesians 4:1 ESV; 2 Timothy 1:9]
11. Does what you are considering come from a pure heart? [1 Samuel 16:7; Luke 6:45]
12. Does what you are considering come from a place of love? [Matthew 22:37–40]

REAL LIFE Questions

1. This chapter suggested that there are four voices a person can listen to: 1-my *own* voice; 2-the voice of *others*; 3-the *enemy's* voice; 4-*God's* voice. Give an example of a time when you heard:

1-your *own* voice _____

2-the voice of *others* _____

3-the *enemy's* voice _____

4-*God's* voice _____

Make some observations about what might block you from being able to hear and discern:

1-your *own* voice _____

2-the voice of *others* _____

3-the *enemy's* voice _____

4-*God's* voice _____

2. Review the twelve questions to help a person *advance* in their decision-making process.

Which one(s) are you already implementing?

_____

_____

Which one(s) would you like to implement more often?

_____

_____

Journal any thoughts related to the questions above.

_____

_____

REAL LIFE Couples Application

Briefly describe a time when you made a decision without including God.

_____

_____

_____

Make some observations regarding specific ways you could have included Him.

_____

_____

_____

How might including Him have impacted the outcome?

_____

_____

_____

Set aside a time/date with your spouse. Together review your answers to the above questions.

_____

_____

_____

Listening to God—I.O.T.L. (*Inquire of the Lord*)

Inviting God into your day by including Him, even in the little things, is one way to build intimacy with Him. Hebrews 12:25 says, "See to it that you do not refuse Him who is speaking." In other words, God *is* speaking, but are you taking the time to listen? At the end of each chapter, we include a *Listening to God* section. This provides an opportunity to *Inquire of the Lord* (I.O.T.L.) and ask the following questions:

+ *Lord, is there anything You want to highlight for me in this section?*

_____

+ *Is there a specific step You want me to take?*

_____

+ *Is there anything You would like me to share with my spouse?*

_____

+ Journal anything you sense the Lord may be saying to you.

_____

_____

CHAPTER 3

WORDS HAVE POWER

Are you familiar with the saying, *sticks and stones may break my bones, but words will never hurt me*? Personally, we do not agree with that statement. In fact, the truth is words can deeply hurt a person and do damage to the relationship. *Why?* Because there is power in words.

James 3:8–11 (TLB) talks about the power of the tongue. It says,

> No human being can tame the tongue. It is always ready to pour out its deadly poison. Sometimes it praises our heavenly Father, and sometimes it breaks out into curses against men who are made like God. And so blessing and cursing come pouring out of the same mouth. Dear brothers, surely this is not right. Does a spring of water bubble out first with fresh water and then with bitter water?

Life Is Lived in a Story

anne

I consider myself a student of life. For me, there are always new things to learn. Since I am also a visual learner, *seeing* something illustrated helps me absorb it faster. For example, there was a season when I was doing a lot of reading about the negative effects shame had on a person's life. I felt like the information was so transformative that I looked for creative ways to illustrate the power that words can have on a person's life. I decided to make truth cards by writing out statements that reinforce a person's God-given identity. For example, some of the cards read, "You are more than enough; you are loved; you are forgiven, and you are chosen." I prayed over each card as I was making them. I asked the Lord to plant these truths deep in my own heart and direct me to those I could share them with.

Socrates, a classical Greek (Athenian) philosopher, was one of the founders of Western philosophy. He is considered the first moral philosopher of the Western ethical tradition. He suggested three penetrating questions regarding when a person speaks, "Is it true; is it kind, or is it necessary?"[1]

As I consider the wisdom in these questions, it encourages me to *think before I speak.* Whether my message is verbal or in the form of a text or email, I ask myself, "*Is what I am about to say true? Is it kind? And is it necessary?*" For me, these three simple questions are such a great reminder that I put them on a letter board and placed it on my kitchen counter as a daily reminder. Tim and I regularly have opportunities to use these questions throughout our day. And as we review the words we speak, too often they are *true* and *necessary*—but not always *kind.*

We challenge you to be intentional and choose words that are *true, kind, necessary—and life-giving*—and to resist speaking to a spouse or others in toxic or destructive ways. Choosing positive, life-giving words strengthens, encourages, and comforts a person. They positively impact community while building relational intimacy. Consider some specific words that were recently said to you. Did they build you up or tear you down?

Words are powerful. The Bible says, "The tongue has the power of life and death."[2] When your words are rooted in the right intention, they can become a prayer you speak over your spouse and others. The Bible says, "The mouth speaks out of that which fills the heart."[3] I want my words to represent my heart. What about *you*—what do *your* words say about what's inside your heart? And are the words you use to communicate a message *true, kind, necessary, and life-giving?*

+ + +

If we go all the way back to creation, *in the beginning,* everything began with the spoken Word. Throughout Genesis it says, "*God said.*" He spoke creation into existence.

> "*God said*, 'Let there be light,' and there was light."[4]
> "*God said*, 'Let there be an expanse in the midst of the waters, and let it separate the waters from the waters.'"[5]

"*God said*, 'Let the waters below the heavens be gathered to one place, and let the dry land appear.'"[6]

"*God said*, 'Let the earth sprout vegetation, plants yielding seed, and fruit trees on the earth bearing fruit after their kind with seed in them.'"[7]

"*God said*, 'Let there be lights in the expanse of the heavens to separate the day from the night, and let them be for signs and for seasons and for days and years, and let them be for lights in the expanse of the heavens to give light on the earth.'"[8]

"*God said*, 'Let the waters teem with swarms of living creatures, and let the birds fly above the earth in the open expanse of the heavens.'"[9]

"*God said*, 'Let the earth bring forth living creatures after their kind: cattle and creeping things beasts of the earth after their kind.'"[10]

"*God blessed them; and God said* to them, 'Be fruitful and multiply, and fill the earth, and subdue it; and rule over the fish in the sea and over the birds of the sky and over every living thing that moves on the earth.'"[11]

"*God said*, 'It is not good for the man to be alone; I will make him a helper suitable for him.'"[12]

When God created men and women in His image and likeness,[13] He gave them the ability to make choices. They can choose obedience or disobedience, to engage or not engage—and to pray or not pray. In addition, every person has freedom to choose the words they speak to a spouse, others, and God. Positive and life-giving words build people up and can become prayers that bless others and even bless the person who prays them. And negative, life-draining words can tear people down and negatively impact them. In marriage, when a husband and wife purposefully speak kind and life-giving words to each other, it results in advancing in intimacy and oneness.

REAL LIFE Questions

1. Read James 3:8–11 out loud. Feel free to compare different translations. What parts of this passage speak to you? Briefly describe.

_____

_____

2. This chapter emphasized that *words have power*. Consider some of the words you have used to describe yourself. Ask the Lord to make you more aware of both negative and positive self-talk. Are the words you use toward yourself kind, gentle, positive, forgiving, and life-giving? Are you harder on yourself than you are on others? Do you ever condemn, blame, or shame yourself?

_____

_____

3. Consider the words you speak to *your spouse*. Are they kind, gentle, positive, forgiving, and life-giving? Or are they condemning? Shaming? Blaming? Make some observations about your answer.

_____

_____

4. Consider the words *your spouse* speaks over themselves. Are they kind, gentle, positive, forgiving, and life-giving? Or are they condemning? Shaming? Blaming? Make some observations about your answer.

_____

_____

Schedule a time/date and together share your answers with one another from this section.

_____

_____

REAL LIFE Couples Application

Review any tendency you may have to speak negative and life-draining words over yourself or your spouse. If you have spoken unkind words and want to ask your spouse for forgiveness, we encourage utilizing our *Forgiveness Model*. Look your spouse directly in the eyes and implement the following three steps:

Step 1— *I am sorry for* [name the specific offense].

Step 2— *I was wrong.*

Step 3— *Will you forgive me?*

[Allow the other person time to respond].[14] Journal any thoughts:

_____

_____

Schedule a time/date and together review your answers to the above question.

_____

_____

Listening to God—I.O.T.L. (*Inquire of the Lord*)

Inviting God into your day by including Him, even in the little things, is one way to build intimacy with Him. Hebrews 12:25 says, "See to it that you do not refuse Him who is speaking." In other words, God *is* speaking, but are you taking the time to listen? At the end of each chapter, we include a *Listening to God* section. This provides an opportunity to *Inquire of the Lord* (**I.O.T.L.**) and ask the following questions:

+ *Lord, is there anything You want to highlight for me in this section?*

_____

+ *Is there a specific step You want me to take?*

_____

+ *Is there anything You would like me to share with my spouse?*

_____

+ Journal anything you sense the Lord may be saying to you.

_____

_____

CHAPTER 4

WHO + WHAT + WHEN + WHY + WHERE OF PRAYER

We have found that it is valuable when engaging in a process, making a decision, or reviewing a topic to ask what are commonly referred to as the *5 W's* (*Who? — What? — When? — Where? — Why?*). Review your prayer life and consider the *5 W's* as they relate to prayer: *Who* should pray? *What* should I pray about? *When* should I pray? *Where* should I pray? *Why* should I pray? Your response to these questions will provide clarity and enable you to advance in intimacy with a spouse, others, and the Lord.

Who Should Pray?

Anyone can pray, but the Bible specially instructs followers of Christ to *pray without ceasing.*[1] In other words, if you are a Christian—you are invited into an ongoing conversation with God—all the time!

What Should a Person Pray?

The Bible says, "Don't worry about anything instead *pray about everything.*"[2] Basically, a person is free to pray about anything—and everything. There are no restrictions or limits. Prayer is a continual conversation with God, an ongoing dialogue that can include specific requests and sharing the desires of your heart. *What* a person chooses to pray is personal to them. They can pray to God, as well as pray for themselves and others.

When Should You Pray?

Certainly, a person can pray whenever they desire. There is no right or wrong time. That said, a best first step is inviting God (I.O.T.L.) into your process and asking the Holy Spirit to provide wisdom and lead you. The Bible makes an amazing promise, "If any of you lacks wisdom, let him ask of God, who gives to all generously and without reproach, and it will be given to him."[3] When it comes to prayer, a person can ask God for wisdom regarding *when* they should pray.

Why Should You Pray?

Why pray? We pray because Jesus prayed.[4] We pray because we want to model our lives after Him. In fact, prayer was so important to Jesus that He taught His disciples to pray.[5] And after praying, Jesus acknowledged that God was listening. He said, "Father, I thank You that You have heard Me."[6] Jesus knew that His followers were human and may lose heart, so He encouraged them to persevere in prayer.[7]

In addition, the apostle Paul recognized the power of prayer and the benefits of including God in every situation. He wrote, "Do not be anxious about anything, but *in every situation*, by prayer and petition, with thanksgiving, present your requests to God. And the peace of God, which transcends all understanding, will guard your hearts and your minds in Christ Jesus."[8] Prayer changes things, and it encourages and motivates people.

Life Is Lived in a Story

tim

Whenever God brings good friends into your life—it's a blessing. Over 20 years ago, we came to Colorado to attend *Wagner Leadership Institute* that met in the *World Prayer Center*. It was there that we met a couple named Jack and Terri. We were not just fellow students; we quickly became friends. As the years passed, our paths continued to cross.

Terri and Jack have played several different roles in our lives. They are friends, intercessors, prayer mentors, and they are pastors who co-lead the church we attend. Like the apostle Paul, in addition to leading our church and numerous prayer gatherings, they are tentmakers who run a painting business in town. As an aside, to give you a visual picture of Jack, he has a booming voice, was a college athlete, is 6 feet 6 inches tall, and wears size 17 shoes! And Terri played college basketball, and she brings that athlete's spirit and discipline to her life—and prayers. *Together*—they are a dynamic couple who are totally sold out to Jesus and advancing God's kingdom.

Anne and I view Jack and Terri as a couple who have left everything to follow Jesus. And they take their call to pray very seriously. They are known throughout Colorado for their gifts of intercession and passion for prayer. As prayer leaders they bring wisdom, insight, and a prophetic voice to our church, this region, and our nation.

It's become a tradition at our church to share *Jesus stories* at the beginning of every gathering. Sharing God sightings is an opportunity to thank God and encourage one another. At a recent weekly church service, Jack shared a story about something that happened to him related to work. And he gave us permission to share it with you. Jack began:

> This week I scheduled one of my crews for a job, and I made arrangements to meet them at the job site. I told them I would stop by the paint store to pick up the supplies they needed for the job. Since the crew was on the clock, I was in a hurry to get the order filled and head to the jobsite. When I walked in the paint store, I noticed the usual team was not there. The only person behind the counter was a young girl I had never met.
>
> She explained to the customers who were waiting with me that the store manager was consulting on a job site and another employee had the day off. She assured us that even though she was new, she was confident that she would be able to mix the paint I needed.
>
> As I watched her begin to mix the paint, I could see that she was struggling with the order. But, instead of correcting her, I wanted to give her the benefit of the doubt. So, I chose to presuppose the best as I thought to myself, *Maybe she just does things in a different order than what I'm used to.* My thought was interrupted as I again remembered that my crew was on the job site—with no paint!
>
> Every time the phone rang, this woman would stop what she was working on to handle the customer on the phone. Time passed by. I found myself becoming more and more impatient as my frustration level continued to increase. I paced back-and-forth in the store. Finally, she finished mixing a gallon of the paint I needed. I asked her to test the paint to make certain it matched the color I needed. When she opened the can, it was obviously not the right tint.

My lack of patience was slowly turning into anger as I found myself silently judging this woman's ability—more accurately *inability*—to mix the paint correctly! So, I decided to leave the store and head to the parking lot so I could manage my emotions. I wasn't sure exactly what to do, so I took a deep breath and began to pray. In my frustration, I asked, "*Lord, why am I waiting so long? Is there something You want me to say—or do?*" After a few moments, I sensed in my heart the Lord response. I walked back in the store and approached the counter where the woman was working.

I leaned toward her and softly said, 'While I was waiting in the parking lot for my order to be completed—I was praying for you. And I felt like God was giving me His heart for you. God simply said, "Tell her I love her." There was a pause as I'm sure my statement caught her by surprise. But as she looked at me, her eyes began to tear up. And after a few moments, she simply said, "*Thank you—that means a lot to me.*"

+ + +

Jack and Terri are people who don't just talk, teach, and preach about prayer—they live a life of prayer. Whenever we're together, we love to hear them share stories related to prayer. Just recently, we were eating breakfast with them in a local restaurant. While we were reading over the menu Jack initiated a conversation with the waitress. He said, "Can I ask, what's the significance of the tattoo on your arm?"

She smiled and said, "It's a DNA strand."

Later, when the waitress brought the bill to our table, Jack quietly leaned over and said to her, "I've been practicing listening to God lately. And I think I heard Him say that the day you were born was a good day for the world. God said that you are unique and special—and He loves you. And He told me your DNA is one-of-a-kind!"

She smiled and thanked him. Before leaving the restaurant, she said to us, "Actually, I recently started working here, and a lot of people have been talking to me about God." When we left, we made sure to leave her a generous tip that reflected the heart of God toward her. I'm sure

Jack and Terri, like most people who listen to God, rarely hear how the stories end. But, when a person focuses on listening to God, it's enough to trust and obey—and trust the end of the story to our trustworthy God.

In the above story, if Jack had not invited God into his story and *listened* to what He sensed in his heart, he would not have had the opportunity to tell a young woman—*God loves you*.

+ + +

Where Should You Pray?

For those who grew up attending church, it's easy to connect prayer with something that is done in church on a particular day of the week. I know that was true for us. We thought the sanctuary provided the atmosphere needed for effective prayer. Growing up, church was a place of safety, security, and protection. Today, if you walk inside a church, it's not unusual to see people praying. In fact, for some people, *where* they pray is as important to them as *what* they pray. We believe churches and sanctuaries are good places to quiet your heart and pray. However, we also agree with Parker Palmer who suggests the sanctuary can be found outside the church,

> When I was a kid, "sanctuary" meant only one thing. It was the big room with the stained-glass windows and hard wooden benches where my family worshiped every Sunday... Today, "sanctuary" is as vital as breathing is to me. Sometimes I find it in churches, monasteries, and other sites formally designated "sacred." But more often I find it in places sacred to my soul: in the natural world, in the company of a faithful friend, in solitary or shared silence, in the ambiance of a good poem or good music. Sanctuary is wherever I find safe space to regain my bearings, reclaim my soul, heal my wounds, and return to the world as a wounded healer.[9]

Since prayer flows out of relationship, talking to God isn't restricted by time or limited to a specific location. A person is free to engage with God wherever and whenever they want. That said, we encourage you to find places where you can refresh your soul and wholeheartedly connect with God.

REAL LIFE Questions

1. Review the 5 W's of prayer: *who, what when, why, where.* Using your own words, briefly respond to the questions below.

Who should pray?

_____

_____

What should you pray?

_____

_____

When should you pray?

_____

_____

Why should you pray?

_____

_____

Where should you pray?

_____

_____

2. Has there ever been a time in your life when you were praying and you sensed God putting someone on your heart? Yes_____ No_____

If yes, how did you respond? Describe the circumstances and outcome.

_____

_____

REAL LIFE Couples Application

Review the 5 W's of prayer: who, what when, where, why with your spouse. Which one(s) are the most challenging for you personally?

_____

_____

Share with your spouse which ones(s) are challenging for you.

_____

_____

What are two ways you can support each other in praying together.

_____

_____

Listening to God—I.O.T.L. (*Inquire of the Lord*)

Inviting God into your day by including Him, even in the little things, is one way to build intimacy with Him. Hebrews 12:25 says, "See to it that you do not refuse Him who is speaking." In other words, God *is* speaking, but are you taking the time to listen? At the end of each chapter, we include a *Listening to God* section. This provides an opportunity to *Inquire of the Lord* (I.O.T.L.) and ask the following questions:

+ *Lord, is there anything You want to highlight for me in this section?*

_____

+ *Is there a specific step You want me to take?*

_____

+ *Is there anything You would like me to share with my spouse?*

_____

+ Journal anything you sense the Lord may be saying to you.

_____

CHAPTER 5

PRAYING WITHOUT CEASING

Life Is Lived in a Story

anne

When I first read 1 Thessalonians 5:17, I was confused. In this passage, Christ followers are instructed to *pray without ceasing*. I remember thinking to myself, *Are there actually people who pray all day—everyday?* More importantly, *Am I supposed to pray all day—every day?* I thought I'd check other translations to see if they might add clarity to what I was reading. The Living Translation reads, "Never stop praying." The Living Bible phrases it this way: "Always keep on praying," and The Message says, "Pray all the time."

Well, doing anything "all the time, non-stop, without ceasing" is not only unrealistic—it's impossible. In my twenties, I remember concluding that this level of spirituality must be reserved for monks in a monastery or cloistered nuns. But certainly not for me. And surely not for the majority of believers in this world.

As the years passed, my perspective on prayer changed in positive ways. Over time, I matured and learned a few things along the way. As I began to trust the Lord with more areas of my life, my relationship with Him grew stronger. And just like any relationship that is advancing in intimacy, a person discovers their desires change along with the relationship. That was certainly true for me.

So, the way I spent time with Him looked a lot different. I wanted to *be* with the Lord throughout my day rather than simply checking off a 15-minute quiet time every morning. I wanted to *know Him* more—and I wanted to be known *by Him*. I longed for my prayer life to be vibrant, active, and moving. Today my life has become an ongoing dialogue with my good Father. A relationship that never ceases because it flows out of my relationship with Him.

This may be easier to understand if I relate the same concept to marriage and the commitment to love a spouse *without ceasing*. In marriage, love is not scheduled or limited by time. Instead, when you love your spouse, it's a relationship that deepens with time—and becomes a practice. Can you imagine the intimacy level in a marriage where a husband or wife schedules 15 minutes with their spouse every morning—and proceeds to do all the talking? Or, what if that spouse recited the same repetitious words, phrases, and requests every single day? That sounds ridiculous doesn't it?

So, at some point I asked myself, "*Why don't some of the same principals for shared intimacy and communication apply to my relationship with God?*" I no longer wanted to just *talk at God* in a one-way conversation—I wanted to relate *with Him*. I wanted to experience the kind of connection that increases intimacy. I came to the realization that I wanted *my life to be my prayer*. As I focus on being *with* God, regular, *ordinary* moments are transformed into *extraordinary* experiences.

From a practical perspective, here's how *praying without ceasing* looks to me. Whatever I am doing, I do it knowing that God is with me. The Bible affirms this saying, "Do you not realize that Christ Jesus is in you...."[1] When I'm driving in the car, He's sitting right next to me. When I'm standing in line at the grocery store, He's standing beside me.

Praying without ceasing isn't a religious activity. It involves ongoing conversations as I relate with a good Father who loves me unconditionally. I view my prayer life not as a monologue, but as a two-way relationship. Of course, I'm still learning, but *praying without ceasing* has become a journey of understanding what it means to *be with God* every moment of my life.

This involves including God in everything...waiting, watching, and listening. *Praying without ceasing* has become a joyful personal and spiritual discipline that helps me "move forward, regardless of circumstances, because God is good—and He is good to me."[2]

+ + +

Life Is Lived in a Story

tim

For me, *praying without ceasing* provides opportunities to connect with God and others. For example, recently, I stopped by the box office at the World Arena near our home. I was purchasing tickets for my daughter, granddaughter, and me to see the Trans-Siberian Orchestra (TSO) Christmas concert. As I got in the box office line, I was again reminded of the Bible text that says, "Do you not realize that Christ Jesus is in you...."[3]

As the Lord and I were standing in line, I observed a middle-aged woman working inside the small securely locked box office. She seemed bored, almost aggravated. As I was waiting, I watched the interactions that were taking place between this woman and the customers who were in line in front of me. As I listened to the conversations they were having, I saw that it wasn't so much *what* they were saying, as it was the *way* they were communicating to this woman. No one smiled, greeted her, or asked her how her day was going. They looked right past her as if her sole purpose in life was to meet their needs as quickly as possible so they could get on with their day.

As I was watching, waiting, and listening, I whispered, *"Lord help me to put a smile on this woman's face."* When it was my turn, I sensed the Lord had given me His heart for this woman. Here she was, locked in this cell-like ticket booth, answering the same questions over-and-over. So, when I stepped up to the window, I looked into her eyes, smiled, and asked her how her day was going. Next, I explained that I wanted three tickets to see Trans-Siberian Orchestra, and I asked if she had ever seen the show. I listened as she briefly described her TSO experience. I told her that I was taking my daughter and granddaughter, and I asked if she thought a 12-year-old would enjoy it. She looked directly into my eyes, took a deep cleansing breath—*smiled*—and said, "She will love it!"

I walked away from the box office thanking the Lord for giving me His heart for a woman I'd most likely never see again. And I especially thanked God for her smile. I asked God if He would bless her in some way that she would know was from Him.

You see, *praying without ceasing* is much more than scheduling a designated time of day to pray. Prayer can happen when you are waking up, getting dressed, showering, or driving to work. Imagine if the routine of getting dressed reminded you to prayerfully ask God to clothe yourself with humility.[4]

A person can pray at work, in the car, grocery store line, restaurant, or when you are picking up a carry-out pizza. Often, when Anne and I are driving to an appointment, we spontaneously pray for the person(s) we are meeting with—that God will give us His heart for them. Our real life experience is as you focus on including God in *every* moment of your life, *your life can become your prayer*.

I continue to be amazed when I slow down and invite God into my life (**I.O.T.L.**). Only God can show me what another person truly needs in a particular moment. As I purposefully include God, He regularly invites me to initiate a conversation and to show interest in someone. And more times than not, it occurs when I ask them about their story.

Truth be told, all too often I live in the smaller story where I inordinately focus on *my* story, *my* narrative—and *my* life is pretty much *all about me*. However, as I try to live in the Larger Story with God as the main character, I am more regularly defaulting to relating to my bride, kids, grandkids, and others in kind and life-giving ways. A simple act of Holy Spirit-led kindness can be a game-changer in turning *ordinary* moments into *extraordinary* moments. And it can become a pathway that provides opportunities to *pray without ceasing*.

Before moving on I suspect some readers may be thinking, *Tim, it sounds like you are an extrovert and a sanguine; relating to people probably comes naturally for you.* My response is to gently push-back and say that introverts, as well as people who lean more toward choleric, phlegmatic, or melancholy personality traits can **I.O.T.L.** and invite God into their relational world. Once again, this involves living in the Larger Story where *God* is the main character— and *it's not about me*. Instead of living in the smaller story where *self* takes center stage—and *it's all about me*.

+ + +

Praying without ceasing[5] can provides ongoing invitations to include God in your life and marriage. For example, we can be working together, counseling, writing, on a date, hiking, and even during intimate moments; these can all become opportunities to invite God into our life and marriage. Prayer positively impacts future generations.

Psalm 78: 1–7 says:

> My people, hear my teaching; listen to the words of my mouth. I will open my mouth with a parable; I will utter hidden things, things from of old—things we have heard and known, things our **ancestors** have told us. We will not hide them from their descendants; we will tell the next generation the praiseworthy deeds of the Lord, his power, and the wonders he has done. He decreed statutes for Jacob and established the law in Israel, which he commanded our ancestors to teach their children, so the next generation would know them, even the children yet to be born, and they in turn would tell their children. Then they would put their trust in God and would not forget his deeds but would keep his commands.

+ + +

We love being grandparents. We consider it such a privilege to pour into them. I (tim) often say, "There are a lot of things in life that are not what they are cracked up to be, but being a grandparent is not on that list!"

It would be great if all of our kids lived near one another. But the reality is we are spread out over Colorado, Michigan, and Texas. So, it's difficult for our entire family to be together as often as we'd like. Of course, we look for every opportunity to call, text, and *FaceTime*. But nothing can replace face-to-face interactions with loved ones.

We also believe it's important to strategically intercede for them, praying specifically for their health and safety and for individual challenges they face. We pray for their teachers, friends, recitals, school tests, church activities, and sporting events. As parents and grandparents, *praying without ceasing*—whether living nearby or far away—is one way to include God in our lives + marriage + family and to hopefully pass on the importance of prayer.

REAL LIFE Questions

1. The Bibles says, pray without ceasing (NASB); never stop praying (Living Translation), always keep on praying (Living Bible), and pray all the time (The Message).[6]
What does pray without ceasing mean to you?

_____

_____

2. Make the decision to reframe praying without ceasing as an ongoing dialogue, a moment-by-moment relationship. Make it a habit to initiate with the Lord—**I.O.T.L.**—throughout your day. Ask your good Father to help you see your spouse, kids, grandkids, and others as He does. Additionally, ask God to give you His heart for them. Journal your thoughts.

_____

_____

REAL LIFE Couples Application

For two weeks agree to focus on praying without ceasing for your spouse. Invite God to show you specific prayers you can pray for him or her. Journal your thoughts.

_____

_____

After two weeks, schedule a time/date and together review how praying without ceasing for your spouse related to advancing in intimacy and spirit + soul + body oneness. Journal any thoughts.

_____

_____

Listening to God—I.O.T.L. (*Inquire of the Lord*)

Inviting God into your day by including Him, even in the little things, is one way to build intimacy with Him. Hebrews 12:25 says, "See to it that you do not refuse Him who is speaking."

In other words, God *is* speaking, but are you taking the time to listen? At the end of each chapter, we include a *Listening to God* section. This provides an opportunity to *Inquire of the Lord* (**I.O.T.L.**) and ask the following questions:

+ *Lord, is there anything You want to highlight for me in this section?*

_____

+ *Is there a specific step You want me to take?*

_____

+ *Is there anything You would like me to share with my spouse?*

_____

+ Journal anything you sense the Lord may be saying to you.

_____

_____

CHAPTER 6

PRAYING INCREASES INTIMACY

Just as human relationships take time to *advance* in intimacy, so does a person's relationship with God. Prayer becomes an ongoing dialogue with the One who longs to be included in *every* area of your life. Consider the progressive relationship between a man and a woman as they move toward marriage. There is a natural rhythm as they transition from *friendship* – to *casual dating* – to *serious dating* – to more advanced steps of *intimacy* – to *engagement* – to *marriage*.

When a person makes intentional choices to *advance* in intimacy, it reflects the desires of their heart. Taking progressive steps indicates a couple wants to experience *more* of something. Perhaps it's *more* commitment, *more* closeness, *more* understanding, *more* safety, *more* intimacy, *more* passionately *living out forgiveness—more love...*

The same is true regarding relationship with God. When a person transitions from viewing God as a distant, impersonal God to viewing Him as a good Father, this results in *advancing* in intimacy. When intentional steps are motivated by a desire for *more* of God, it changes the way a person relates to God. And as a person *advances* in intimacy with God, it impacts the ways they pray.

The more you know God, the more your heart is impacted and your love for Him grows. The more you love God, the more you trust Him. And the more you trust Him, the more you want to share your life with Him. Relating to prayer, as your intimacy with God increases, you begin to discover that your ongoing relationship with God throughout day-to-day interactions can become prayers.

Prayer softens a person's heart and creates space for God to speak. And when a person's heart is sensitive to God, whatever He may be inviting them to do is much more important than anything they have planned.

Life Is Lived in a Story

tim+anne

When we create space to listen to God, we tend to respond to life circumstances with prayer. Growing up in families that modeled prayer positively impacted us. And as grateful as we are for the model our families provided, we wanted a more personal connection. As we experienced God in deeper ways, we learned to trust Him more. For us, responding to life with prayer is an act of faith and a practice of surrender. We invite God into our story, and when we do, it changes the way we pray.

As we continue to walk through life, we are reminded of how much is outside of our control. There have been times when we were watching the evening news and our hearts were tugged by one of the stories. Whether it's personal or political, our response is to pray. For example, we recall the story about a coach and young soccer team from Taiwan who were trapped in a cave that was filling with water. We have never been to that part of the world, and we didn't have a relationship with anyone in that story. But when we heard the report, we felt such a strong burden from the Lord to pray for these children and their coach, that they would be safe and successfully rescued.

We also believe the story God is telling through a person's life influences the way they pray. For example, after serving over twenty years in the fire service, I (tim) continually feel prompted to pray when I hear stories that involve first responders. Whenever I hear about a fire, emergency incident, mass shooting, international pandemic, or any trauma related to the fire or police department—I pray. In fact, whenever I hear an emergency vehicle siren blaring—I pray.

There have also been nights when we were awakened from a sound sleep and God placed a person, situation, or circumstance on our hearts. It may be something that is *currently* happening, something that has *already* happened, or we ask God to *prevent* something from happening. Instead of giving in to anxiety, worry, or fear—we pray. We ask God to intervene, protect, rescue, restore, and heal.

As we focus on the Bible passage that commands, "Take captive every thought to make it obedient to Christ,"[1] and as we focus on listening to the Holy Spirit, we are surprised how often the names of specific people and circumstances come to mind. Initially, we may not know exactly *how* to pray or *what* to pray—but we trust that God will lead us. Listening prayer supernaturally connects us to our good Father and reveals His heart to us. As this occurs, the key is to respond with a "yes" spirit—*and to pray.*

REAL LIFE Questions

1. Do you believe God still speaks? Yes_____ No_____ Explain your answer.

_____

_____

2. The Bible says, "Be careful that you do not refuse to listen to the One who is speaking."[2] Share a time when you listened to God. What were the circumstances, and what was the outcome?

_____

_____

3. Advancing in listening skills creates space for God to speak and for you to listen. What are two ways you can intentionally make space for God to speak—as you listen?

_____

_____

_____

REAL LIFE Couples Application

When a person makes choices to advance in intimacy, it reflects desires of their heart. In marriage, taking progressive steps indicates a couple wants to experience more of something. Perhaps it's more commitment, more closeness, more understanding, more safety, more intimacy, more extending forgiveness—more love...

Husbands and wives who are committed to each other and are willing to listen and pray become more sensitive to the Spirit of God. These kinds of intentional choices help couples advance in intimacy with God—and with each other.

List two ways you can purposefully advance in listening to God as a couple.

_____

_____

Schedule a time/date and together review your answers to the above questions. Set aside a time to practice what you are learning.

_____

_____

Listening to God—I.O.T.L. (*Inquire of the Lord*)

Inviting God into your day by including Him, even in the little things, is one way to build intimacy with Him. Hebrews 12:25 says, "See to it that you do not refuse Him who is speaking." In other words, God **is** speaking, but are you taking the time to listen? At the end of each chapter, we include a *Listening to God* section. This provides an opportunity to *Inquire of the Lord* (**I.O.T.L.**) and ask the following questions:

+ *Lord, is there anything You want to highlight for me in this section?*

_____

+ *Is there a specific step You want me to take?*

_____

+ *Is there anything You would like me to share with my spouse?*

_____

+ Journal anything you sense the Lord may be saying to you.

_____

_____

CHAPTER 7

PRAYER AND GOD'S WILL

Life Is Lived in a Story

tim

There have been many times throughout years of counseling when someone will ask, *"How can I know God's will for my life?"* I respond by opening the Bible to 1 Thessalonians 5:16–18. This passage offers a simple response to this seemingly complex question. It says, *"Rejoice always; pray without ceasing; in everything give thanks; for this is God's will for you in Christ Jesus."*[1] Can you envision this portion of Scripture becoming a prayer?

Father, give me a heart that is willing to:

+ *Rejoice always*

+ *Pray without ceasing*

+ *In everything give thanks*

Imagine God's will for your life becoming an ongoing prayer, it might sound something like this:

Father, open the eyes of my heart. Show me things I may tend to overlook or take for granted. Help me to live with greater joy as I look for ways to **rejoice** *always. Lord, my desire is to live in the Larger Story and include You in every area of my life—and to* **pray** *about everything. Remind me to* **give thanks** *throughout my day. Thank You, Father, for unconditionally loving me and never giving up on me...*

In our experience, purposefully living out God's will—*rejoicing + praying + giving thanks*—helps us *advance* in intimacy and whole-heartedly live out our calling as *missionaries to marriage.*

+ + +

Praying Persistently

In addition to living out *God's will*, another key to *advancing* in prayer is being persistent—*and not giving up*. Following is the biblical story that is referred to as *The Parable of the Persistent Widow.*[2] The text reads:

> Then Jesus told his disciples a parable to show them that they should always pray and not give up. He said: "In a certain town there was a judge who neither feared God nor cared what people thought. And there was a widow in that town who kept coming to him with the plea, 'Grant me justice against my adversary.'
>
> "For some time he refused. But finally he said to himself, 'Even though I don't fear God or care what people think, yet because this widow keeps bothering me, I will see that she gets justice, so that she won't eventually come and attack me!'"
>
> And the Lord said, "Listen to what the unjust judge says. And will not God bring about justice for his chosen ones, who cry out to him day and night? Will he keep putting them off? I tell you, he will see that they get justice, and quickly. However, when the Son of Man comes, will he find faith on the earth?"

Life Is Lived in a Story

tim

Following is a modern-day version of the *Persistent Widow* story. A friend in our church is a passionate intercessor, and he is also a die-hard *Kansas City Royals* baseball fan. He is such a major fan that I respectfully nicknamed him "Royal." A while back, he shared with me the following real life story that illustrates the principles of following your dreams, being persistent, and *never giving up!*

> Back in the day you could catch the bus at the *Gold Buffet* restaurant in North Kansas City and for one dollar and fifty cents ride unsupervised to and from *Kauffman Stadium—home of the Kansas City Royals*. If one was wily of mind and heart, they could buy an inexpensive general admission ticket, strategically navigate around the ushers, execute a daring escape from your *cheap-seat* and relocate to an expensive *box-seat*

all by the start of the 5th inning! Whenever I sat in that ballpark, as I took everything in, I'd find myself passionately joining thousands of *Royal* fans singing the *Royals*-rally-chant ... *here we go Royals—here we go—(clap-clap!) ... here we go Royals—here we go—(clap-clap!)*.

At 12 years old, going to the ballpark and cheering for the *Royals* was my favorite way to spend summer evenings. At one particular game, during the 7th inning stretch, I found a *Royals* program and noticed the equipment manager's name was Al Zych. I put two-and-two together, and I made a call to the *Royals* administrative office. Somehow, I charmed the operator into giving me Al Zych's home phone number. Well, I probably fibbed a little bit to get it, truth-be-told it was nearly 40 years ago, and I can neither confirm nor deny remembering our exact conversation verbatim!

Since I had his phone number, on the first day of every month I phoned Al Zych at home and said, "*Will you please let me be the Royals batboy?*" At some point everybody in his home recognized my voice. Typically, after one of his kids answered, I would hear them holler; "Hey Dad, it's that dude who keeps bugging you for the batboy job."

Six years later, after calling him on the first day of every month, he finally said, "Okay, you've worn me down, meet me at the ballpark tomorrow 2 pm—sharp!" I met with Mr. Zych, and he offered me the *Kansas City Royals* batboy job! As I left the ballpark, I clutched my brand-new major league *Royals* uniform to my chest, and I thought to myself, "*I'm on my team—I AM A KANSAS CITY ROYAL!*" And I cried tears of joy.

None of my friends believed me until they saw me in my *Royals* uniform at the home opener. In fact, you can find me on the 1979 *Kansas City Royals* team card, front and center. I'm the batboy with curly blonde hair.

As a batboy, I picked up bats that were used by major league All-Stars and future hall-of-fame players. I brought countless baseballs to umpires. I never missed a game. I never missed an inning. I would not have had it any other way! Sometimes I would slap myself and think, "*I am on the Kansas City Royals baseball field! I am standing next to an emerging baseball legend, George Brett (#5) as he walks up to the plate. Royals ace Paul Splittorff (#34) is on the pitcher's mound! And Hal McRae (#11) is making another game-saving catch in the outfield!*"

In the mid-seventies, there were epic playoff battles between my beloved *K.C. Royals* and the legendary *New York Yankees*. After three first place finishes, I traded my *Royals* jersey in for a missionary knapsack and I traveled the globe. Whether I was in the jungles of South America, on the 23rd floor of an Asian skyscraper, or on a tiny Greek island in the Mediterranean, I always tried to find a way to know what inning my *Royals* were in, the score, and who was on base!

Some days after a tough loss was taking a toll on me, my wife would attempt to lovingly console me, saying, "Honey, I know you love the Royals—but unfortunately you're not on the team anymore." Of course, she was right, I was not on the team. But in my mind, I could still picture myself as a teenager at the ballpark wearing my *Kansas City Royals* uniform.

And even to this day, if I close my eyes I can feel like I'm back at the ballpark. I can smell the infield grass and hear the one-of-a-kind sound of a bat jacking a fastball into the grandstands. And as I do this, I find myself once again singing the *Royals*-rally-chant ... *here we go Royals—here we go—(clap-clap!) ... here we go Royals—here we go—(clap-clap!)*.

Stop for a moment and think about my friend's persistence. On the first day of the month—*for six years*—he phoned the equipment manager and begged him to let him be the *Royals* batboy. It makes me wonder, "*What if my friend had given up on his dream and stopped calling after 5 years?*" Think about everything he would have missed out on.

All that is to say, *How about you?* Like the persistent widow and *Royal*, are you unyielding in pursuing your dreams as you follow the passions in your heart—or are you quick to throw in the towel and give up?

REAL LIFE Questions

1. Read out loud 1 Thessalonians 5:16–18, "*Rejoice* always; *pray* without ceasing; in *everything give thanks*; for this is God's will for you in Christ Jesus."

What is one way you *rejoice*?

_____

_____

What is one way you observe *your spouse rejoicing*?

_____

_____

What is one way *you pray*?

_____

_____

What is one way you observe *your spouse praying*?

_____

_____

What is one way *you give thanks*?

_____

_____

2. Re-read *Royal's* batboy story. How did you feel after you read it? Did it remind you of any dreams you may have forgotten—or given up on? Journal any thoughts.

_____

_____

REAL LIFE Couples Application

As you consider God's will for your marriage, what does *rejoicing + praying + giving thanks* currently look like for you?

_____

_____

List two ways that you are willing to practice *rejoicing + praying + giving thanks* in your marriage?

_____

_____

Schedule a time/date and together review your answers to the above questions.

_____

_____

Listening to God—I.O.T.L. (*Inquire of the Lord*)

Inviting God into your day by including Him, even in the little things, is one way to build intimacy with Him. Hebrews 12:25 says, "See to it that you do not refuse Him who is speaking." In other words, God *is* speaking, but are you taking the time to listen? At the end of each chapter, we include a *Listening to God* section. This provides an opportunity to *Inquire of the Lord* (**I.O.T.L.**) and ask the following questions:

+ *Lord, is there anything You want to highlight for me in this section?*

_____

+ *Is there a specific step You want me to take?*

_____

+ *Is there anything You would like me to share with my spouse?*

_____

+ Journal anything you sense the Lord may be saying to you.

_____

_____

CHAPTER 8

LIST PRAYING

Life Is Lived in a Story

tim

If you asked my family or those who know me well to describe me, I suspect they would say I tend to be a goal-oriented, structured person. Coming from a para-military fire department career, I've always been drawn to a disciplined lifestyle. I am one of those people who likes to make lists and check things off when they've been completed.

In fact, that transfers over to my prayer life. I am what you call a "list-pray-*er*." My list helps me to live out the Bible passage that says, "Devote yourselves to prayer."[1] Occasionally, I sense God inviting me to add a person to my prayer list. Or, when someone asks me to pray, I like to check with God first—**I.O.T.L.**—and if I'm led, I add them to my prayer list.

For me, the discipline of prayer is an important part of my life. I pray over my list pretty much every day. I specifically pray for my marriage, kids, grandkids, spiritual kids, and that God's creational marriage design is reclaimed. I regularly cry out to God for marriage transformation, for marriage reformation, for REAL LIFE ministries, and for our call to be *missionaries to marriage*. I pray for friends, mentors, ministry partners, leaders, churches, and a number of parachurch ministries.

My prayer list includes praying Scripture and making specific declarations. For example, I have an old note card attached to my prayer list that is dated May 11, 2004. On it I wrote out Job 42, and pretty much every day I pray out loud parts of versus 8 through 16. Like Job, my prayer includes asking God to accept my prayers and to bless me with resources so I can generously bless others. I ask God to bless the latter part of my life more than the former, to give lots of biological and spiritual sons and daughters to Anne and me; and to enable me to see them to the fourth generation.

I also pray for our nation, especially as I think about the weight of leadership. I pray in agreement with the Bible passage that reads, "I urge you, first of all, to pray for all people. Ask God to help them; intercede on their behalf, and give thanks for them. Pray this way for kings and all who are in authority so that we can live peaceful and quiet lives marked by godliness and dignity. This is good and pleases God our Savior, who wants everyone to be saved and to understand the truth."[2] For years I have specifically prayed for our Democrat or Republican Presidents—especially for their marriage and family. I also pray for court judges and justices and local and national political leaders.

In addition to leaders, my prayer list includes celebrities and athletes. For example, decades ago I sensed God inviting me to pray for Oprah. At the time, I considered her talk show audience *figuratively speaking* to be one of the largest churches in America. When Pope Frances began his papacy, I felt committed to pray for him. I've prayed for a specific NFL quarterback and have declared Proverbs 3:5–6 over him since his college days. And long after retiring as Deputy Fire Chief, I continue to pray for the Schaumburg Fire Department. To this day, there are specific firemen and their spouses I feel led to pray for by name.

I love this quote by Max Lucado, "Our prayers may be awkward. Our attempts may be feeble. But since the power of prayer is in the one who hears it and not in the one who says it, our prayers do make a difference."[3] When I consider my prayer list, I'm thankful it isn't dependent on my relationship with the person I am praying for. My prayers are my heart's response to my relationship with God.

Prayer is not something I *have* to do; it's something I *get* to do. And as I look back over many years, I truly believe praying for the things on my prayer list makes a difference. The Bible says, "The prayer of a person living right with God is something powerful to be reckoned with."[4] For me, prayer has changed from a disciplined 15-minute quiet time at the beginning of my day to an ongoing moment-by-moment dialogue with my good Father.

REAL LIFE Questions

1. Have you ever used a list to help you pray? Yes_____ No_____

If yes, what were the benefits of praying over your list?

_____

_____

If No, do you think a list could give you a more specific prayer focus? Yes_____ No_____

If Yes, would you be willing to try it for a month? Yes _____ No _____

2. Write down some prayer requests you would include on your list?

_____

_____

REAL LIFE Couples Application

The Bible says. "The prayer of a person living right with God is something powerful to be reckoned with."[5] Take some time and together with your spouse develop a marriage prayer list. Write out a few specific prayers that will help you advance in intimacy (be specific) and commit to praying over it individually and as a couple.

_____

_____

_____

Schedule a time/date and review how praying your marriage list impacted you, your marriage, and your advancing in intimacy.

_____

_____

_____

Listening to God—I.O.T.L. (*Inquire of the Lord*)

Inviting God into your day by including Him, even in the little things, is one way to build intimacy with Him. Hebrews 12:25 says, "See to it that you do not refuse Him who is speaking." In other words, God *is* speaking, but are you taking the time to listen? At the end of each chapter, we include a *Listening to God* section. This provides an opportunity to *Inquire of the Lord* (**I.O.T.L.**) and ask the following questions::

+ *Lord, is there anything You want to highlight for me in this section?*

_____

+ *Is there a specific step You want me to take?*

_____

+ *Is there anything You would like me to share with my spouse?*

_____

+ Journal anything you sense the Lord may be saying to you.

_____

_____

CHAPTER 9

PRAYING SCRIPTURE

In addition to list praying, another way to advance in intimacy with your good Father is to strategically use the Bible—the Word of God—as a prayer guide. The Bible provides wisdom, strength, and direction. It is divinely inspired and a guide that can be used as a form of prayer. Hebrews 4:12 reminds us, "The word of God is living and active and sharper than any two-edged sword." When a person opens up the Scriptures and declares God's Word over a person or situation, it can be a form of prayer.

Life Is Lived in a Story

anne+tim

Years ago, we were pastors of prayer at a local church in Holland, Michigan. During that time, we had the privilege of being exposed to many different styles of prayer. And we made it a priority to regularly join a prayer group that included a number of local church leaders. It was at that prayer meeting that we began to experience the power of praying Scriptures.

Here is how it worked, people would begin by declaring out loud a verse or portion of the Bible. This was followed by conversational prayer that personalized what was read. It sounded something like this:

> + "Father, Matthew chapter 7 verse 7 says, '*Ask, and it will be given to you; seek, and you will find; knock, and it will be opened to you.*' Father, we are *asking*, we are *seeking*, we are *knocking* on the door of your heart. Father, we are asking for a miracle. Will You turn the hearts of the people in this city toward You? And will You soften the hearts of those whose hearts have become hard?"

> + "Your Word says in Romans chapter 2 verse 4b, '*The kindness of God leads you to repentance.*' Lord, please impact people's lives, marriages, and families with Your kindness as You lovingly lead them to repentance."

+ "Lord, Proverbs 3:5-6 (TLB) says, '*If you want favor with both God and man, and a reputation for good judgment and common sense, then trust the Lord completely; don't ever trust yourself. In everything you do, put God first, and he will direct you and crown your efforts with success.*' Father, we trust You, and we want to be people who put You first in everything. Lord, will You give us the humility to focus on You rather than on ourselves and our desires? In fact, Lord will You replace our desires with Your desires?"

Another example of praying a specific Scripture:

+ "Second Peter chapter 3 verse 9 reminds us, '*You are not slow about Your promise, as some count slowness, but patient, not wishing for any to perish but for all to come to repentance.*' Lord, based on the promises of Your Word, we pray for our family and friends by name, [specific names]. Father, we declare Your love and this passage over them..."

+ + +

Life Is Lived in a Story

anne

Counseling for many decades, Tim and I have seen how destructive anxiety can be in a person's life. Clients often describe ways the enemy robs them of God's peace. Anxiety can be a mental and emotional distraction that blocks a person from being able to live in the present. In recent years, Tim and I have seen an increasing number of clients who struggle with anxiety. Their symptoms range from mild to severe.

Anxiety can be addressed in a variety of ways, including managing stress levels, sleep, exercise, nutrition, breathing, tapping, meditating, and medication. While these can all be valuable tools, it's also important to address anxiety from a spiritual perspective. We challenge people who struggle with anxiety to make it a practice to renew their minds[1] and focus on their true identity—who God says they are. Another way to deal with anxiety from a spiritual perspective is to put on the full armor of God:

Finally, be strong in the Lord and in his mighty power. Put on the full armor of God, so that you can take your stand against the devil's schemes. For our struggle is not against flesh and blood, but against the rulers, against the authorities, against the powers of this dark world and against the spiritual forces of evil in the heavenly realms. Therefore put on the full armor of God, so that when the day of evil comes, you may be able to stand your ground, and after you have done everything, to stand. Stand firm then, with the belt of truth buckled around your waist, with the breastplate of righteousness in place, and with your feet fitted with the readiness that comes from the gospel of peace. In addition to all this, take up the shield of faith, with which you can extinguish all the flaming arrows of the evil one. Take the helmet of salvation and the sword of the Spirit, which is the word of God.[2]

When people implement the above steps and put on the full armor of God, they often report how it positively impacts their struggle with anxiety. *Are you up for a challenge?* If you struggle with anxiety, declare the following Scripture over yourself for 30 days. "Rejoice in the Lord always. I will say it again: Rejoice! Let your gentleness be evident to all. The Lord is near. *Do not be anxious about anything, but in every situation, by prayer and petition, with thanksgiving*, present your requests to God. And the *peace of God*, which transcends all understanding, will guard your hearts and your minds in Christ Jesus."[3]

Praying Scripture as a Couple

Over the years, married couples have asked us how to start praying together. One of the models we suggest is to start by praying in agreement with Scripture. Simply choose one verse as a focus and go back and forth with short sentences praying in agreement, plus adding any related requests. Couples who pray Scripture together have given us lots of positive feedback. They describe how, using Scripture as their framework, they were able to pray with a shared focus. Praying Scripture also helped them to store God's Word in their hearts.[4]

Praying Scripture allows a person to stand on God's promises. Early in our marriage we purchased prayer books that highlighted specific Scriptures to help us pray. And after decades of marriage, we continue to confidently declare God's Word over ourselves, each other, our marriage, our family, our friends, our ministry, and our *missionaries to marriage* calling.

REAL LIFE Questions

1. List two of your favorite Bible passages. Pray them out loud.

_____

_____

2. What are a few benefits of praying these Scriptures out loud?

_____

_____

3. Review Philippians 4:4–7. How do you think being anxious can relate to experiencing God's peace?

_____

_____

REAL LIFE Couples Application

Invite the Holy Spirit to lead you in praying together. Open your Bible, choose a portion of Scripture that speaks to both of your hearts, then pray it together out loud. Remember, you have total freedom to personalize your prayers. When you are finished, share with your spouse how you felt after finishing this challenge.

_____

_____

_____

_____

_____

Listening to God—I.O.T.L. (*Inquire of the Lord*)

Inviting God into your day by including Him, even in the little things, is one way to build intimacy with Him. Hebrews 12:25 says, "See to it that you do not refuse Him who is speaking." In other words, God *is* speaking, but are you taking the time to listen? At the end of each chapter, we include a *Listening to God* section. This provides an opportunity to *Inquire of the Lord* (**I.O.T.L.**) and ask the following questions:

+ *Lord, is there anything You want to highlight for me in this section?*

_____

+ *Is there a specific step You want me to take?*

_____

+ *Is there anything You would like me to share with my spouse?*

_____

+ Journal anything you sense the Lord may be saying to you.

_____

_____

CHAPTER 10

PRAYER AND SPIRITUAL WARFARE

Life can be hard. The Bible says that when you experience trials, the testing of your faith will produce endurance.[1] This passage does not say *if* you experience trials; it says *when* you experience them. And if you are married, the Bible clearly says that every couple "will have trouble in this life."[2] But the good news is the *testing of your faith* has the potential to mature you and give you endurance.[3]

When the Bible talks about *struggles*, it uses some strong language that to us sounds a lot like engaging in warfare. For example, Ephesians 6:12 says, "For our struggle is not against flesh and blood, but against the rulers, against the powers, against the world forces of this darkness, against the spiritual forces of wickedness in the heavenly places."

The battle that rages between good and evil can be referred to as *spiritual warfare*. And one of the most effective weapons used in spiritual warfare is prayer. We suspect readers have a number of different responses when they hear the term *spiritual warfare*. Some people may relate spiritual warfare to a battle of good versus evil. For others spiritual warfare may conjure up scenes from *The Exorcist* or images of TV deliverance ministers yelling and casting out demons. And for others, the term *spiritual warfare* may invoke images of angels battling demons in cosmic battles in the heavenlies.

Regardless of what you call it—*there are battles going on between good and evil*. The reality is every human being lives in a world that includes both real life and spiritual struggles, and marriage is no exception. Therefore, wisely engaging in spiritual warfare is an opportunity for husbands and wives to say, "We recognize there are battles in life, especially related to our marriage and family, and we are willing to fight for our marriage. And one way we will do this is through focused prayer."

We suspect some readers may be shaking their heads and thinking, *Dark forces, good and evil—are you serious?* Although we do not have a lot of information on the beginnings of evil, we believe evil exists. The Bible describes that at a point in time a group of spiritual beings rebelled against God. This rebellious coup had a leader named Satan. This being does not dress in a red cape or have horns and a pitchfork. But he does exist.

Satan is real, and Jesus acknowledged his existence.[4] Furthermore, his nature and character are described in the Bible. He is a creature.[5] He is a spirit being.[6] He is of the order of the angels called cherubim.[7] He was the highest of all angelic creatures.[8] His personality traits include murderer,[9] liar,[10] confirmed sinner ,[11] accuser,[12] and adversary.[13] He also knows and uses the Word of God.[14] Satan and his cohorts have a clear mission. They are committed to stealing, killing, and destroying. "The thief comes only to *steal* and *kill* and *destroy*; I [Jesus] came that they may have life, and have it abundantly."[15]

We've been believers in God our entire lives. But in all honesty, for a good portion of our lives we never thought much about spiritual warfare. We were taught to live out the Great Commandment—to wholeheartedly love God, others, and ourselves.[16] And we focused on living out the golden rule by treating people in the ways we wanted to be treated. We prayed, served at church, and gave our time, talents, and treasures. But growing up, we did not hear much about spiritual warfare in church. So, we came to the conclusion on our own that if the devil did exist, he was *not* someone you wanted to mess with.

However, over the years we have learned that God has given every one of His followers a measure of spiritual authority. Unfortunately, our experience is this authority is often denied, discounted, or overlooked. Stop for a moment and review how Jesus responded to spiritual warfare and to the demonic realm. Jesus understood the battle between good and evil. In fact, after His baptism the Holy Spirit led Him into the wilderness for a power encounter where Satan tempted Him. Consider this, if Satan did not possess the authority to give Jesus the things he offered, it would not have been a true temptation.[17] Yet, Jesus as a human being stepped into the authority God had given Him and responded to the enemy's temptations.

If, like us, you did not grow up learning about the demonic realm and spiritual warfare, we encourage you to study the Gospels. Highlight the times when Jesus encountered Satan and demons, and observe His responses. Even when Jesus taught His disciples to pray, He included in the Lord's prayer, "Deliver us from evil...."[18]

Often when people talk about the demonic world and spiritual warfare, they take one of four positions. They either:

1- *Deny* the reality of demons and spiritual warfare.
2- *Fear* the demonic.
3- Become *fascinated* with it.
4- *Focus on the authority they have in Jesus Christ* and prayerfully engage in spiritual warfare as the Holy Spirit leads.

In our experience, one of the main weapons the devil and demons default to is fear, which they use to manipulate, intimidate, and control. Regarding fear, followers of Christ should guard their hearts[19] and renounce and reject fear. The apostle Paul commanded the Corinthian church regarding Timothy, "See to it that he has nothing to fear while he is with you, for he is carrying on the work of the Lord, just as I am."[20] Another passage says. "There is no fear in love. But perfect love drives out fear."[21]

After guarding your heart, renouncing and rejecting fear, and focusing on love, it's essential to understand that Christ-followers have authority and power—*in the name and blood of Jesus Christ of Nazareth*—to defeat the enemies' schemes. The Bible says; "...The one who is in you is greater than the one who is in the world."[22]

The truth is, there is a spiritual dynamic to life that the Bible describes as rulers, powers, world forces of darkness, and spiritual forces of wickedness in heavenly places.[23] These beings are committed to doing everything they can to *steal* and *kill* and *destroy*.[24] Their mission includes wreaking havoc, inhibiting intimacy, and destroying marriages and families. Thankfully, the Bible brings good news declaring that Jesus came so that we may have life and have it abundantly.[25]

Before moving on, if things we have written about in this chapter have stirred up questions for you, we encourage you to study the Bible and review how Jesus dealt with evil and demons. Take some time to observe our world and ask yourself, *Is it possible for a person to think that evil does not exist?* Review your positions regarding good versus evil and spiritual warfare. And consider talking to people who have a measure of expertise in these areas, because "in the abundance of counselors there is victory."[26]

REAL LIFE Questions

Read out loud Ephesians 6:12, which says, "For our struggle is not against flesh and blood, but against the rulers, against the powers, against the world forces of this darkness, against the spiritual forces of wickedness in the heavenly places."

How do *you* describe spiritual warfare?

_____

_____

_____

How do you think *your spouse* would describe spiritual warfare?

_____

_____

_____

2. Have you ever experienced spiritual warfare? If *yes*, what were the circumstances, and how did you respond?

_____

_____

_____

3. Often when people talk about the demonic world and spiritual warfare, they take one of four positions. They either: *Deny* the reality of demons and spiritual warfare. *Fear* the demonic. Become *fascinated* with it. Or *focus on the authority they have in Jesus Christ*, as they prayerfully engage in spiritual warfare as the Holy Spirit leads. Which of these would you typically default to? Journal any thoughts.

_____

_____

_____

4. If you tend to deny, fear, or are fascinated with the demonic world, what are two things you can purposefully do to step into the authority you have in Jesus Christ and engage in spiritual warfare as the Holy Spirit leads you?

_____

_____

_____

REAL LIFE Couples Application

Talk with your spouse about some of the trials that have tested your faith throughout your marriage. How have these produced endurance in you (James 1:2–4)? How have they impacted your marriage?

_____

_____

_____

_____

_____

Listening to God—I.O.T.L. (*Inquire of the Lord*)

Inviting God into your day by including Him, even in the little things, is one way to build intimacy with Him. Hebrews 12:25 says, "See to it that you do not refuse Him who is speaking." In other words, God *is* speaking, but are you taking the time to listen? At the end of each chapter, we include a *Listening to God* section. This provides an opportunity to *Inquire of the Lord* (**I.O.T.L.**) and ask the following questions:

+ *Lord, is there anything You want to highlight for me in this section?*

_____

_____

+ *Is there a specific step You want me to take?*

_____

_____

+ *Is there anything You would like me to share with my spouse?*

_____

_____

+ Journal anything you sense the Lord may be saying to you.

_____

_____

CHAPTER 11

STRATEGIC PRAYER

Life Is Lived in a Story

anne

Growing up in a religious home, I memorized a number of traditional prayers, including *The Lord's Prayer*, *Hail Mary*, *Apostles Creed*, *Act of Contrition*, and saying *Grace* at meal times. In fact, if you asked me today, I could still recite each of these prayers out loud. As I grew in my relationship with God, my desire to talk to Him became more intimate. After a lifetime of praying the same prayers, I recall a season when I decided to stop praying them. At that time, I thought they lacked authenticity. My heart's desire was that my conversations with God would be more personal, so I used my own words.

Throughout years of walking with the Lord, my relationship with Him continues to grow. And my view of praying the same prayers over-and-over has changed. I've come to view them as strategic and powerful. Today, when I pray a traditional prayer, I know it can encompass much more than I might pray on my own.

+ + +

Life Is Lived in a Story

tim

When we served as pastors of prayer at a local church, we noticed that whenever people prayed, their prayers were almost always related to emotional and physical health issues and concerns. The Bible says, "Take delight in the Lord, and he will give you the *desires of your heart*."[1] For many people, having *good health* is at or near the top of the *desires of their heart*.

The Bible also says, "You do not have because you do not ask God."[2] As a good Father, God loves to hear prayer requests from *beloved* sons and daughters. Picture a small child leaping into their grandmother or grandfather's arms with total joy and trust.

That said, it takes a measure of faith to ask God for the desires of your heart. *Why?* Our counseling experiences suggest that all too often people are hesitant to ask for things because there is always the possibility of being disappointed. But as a person's faith grows, their trust in God grows deeper, and their focus shifts from getting things they want to *advancing* in intimacy. For some people, a written prayer can address issues more specifically than a prayer a person might pray on their own.

Praying Out Loud

As an aside, when we lead REAL LIFE gatherings on *Prayer*, during the question-and-answer time a person often asks, "Why should I pray out loud?" On the one hand, the Bible warns those who enjoy praying out loud in front of others:

> And when you pray, do not be like the hypocrites, for they love to pray standing in the synagogues and on the street corners to be seen by others. Truly I tell you, they have received their reward in full. But when you pray, go into your room, close the door and pray to your Father, who is unseen. Then your Father, who sees what is done in secret, will reward you. And when you pray, do not keep on babbling like pagans, for they think they will be heard because of their many words.[3]

So why pray out loud? For us, praying out loud is making a formal declaration to God—and to the enemy. We consider declarations as a form of spiritual warfare. Remember, God hears your prayers before you even ask Him. The Bible affirms this saying," For your Father knows what you need before you ask him."[4] Praying out loud builds our faith, renews our minds, and repositions us to receive. Praying out loud reminds us that our allegiance and trust rests in God—and we are not defined by our circumstances. Praying out loud symbolizes the two-way relationship that exists between us and our good God. It's a reminder to surrender our plans and any anxieties.

A part of the good news is that God hears our prayers even when we don't know how or what to pray.

Meanwhile, the moment we get tired in the waiting, God's Spirit is right alongside helping us along. If we don't know how or what to pray, it doesn't matter. He does our praying in and for us, making prayer out of our wordless sighs, our aching groans. He knows us far better than we know ourselves, knows our pregnant condition, and keeps us present before God. That's why we can be so sure that every detail in our lives of love for God is worked into something good.[5]

✝ ✝ ✝

Following is a prayer that focuses on health and wholeness. We encourage you make this prayer a declaration by praying it out loud.

Prayer for Health and Wholeness

In the power of God, the Holy Spirit, and in the name of Jesus Christ, I ask that You bless me with health and wholeness. Remove all stress, anxiety, fear, trauma, sickness, cancer cells, calcifications, or diseases from my body.

I pray you bless my mind, body, cells, blood stream, and DNA. Restore my organs to their normal function, including my heart, lungs, liver, stomach, esophagus, kidneys, prostate gland, muscles, ligaments, tendons, joints, cartilage, bones, and bone marrow. Protect my nervous system—from my brain stem to every nerve ending. Bless my cardiovascular, endocrine, lymphatic, digestive, and musculoskeletal systems.

In Jesus name, I declare Your healing over any cancers, heart problems, coronary artery disease, lung issues, diabetes, dementia, or Alzheimer's disease. I declare healing to all trauma and injuries to my body, mind, and soul—including anxiety, depression, shock, trauma, and PTSD.

In Jesus' name, I ask You to cancel any assignments of the enemy. Reverse any ungodly thoughts, beliefs, or generational propensities. I renounce and reject every scheme of the enemy; I reject all word curses; I reject all fears—including the fear of death, disease, sickness, trauma, and unfulfilled dreams. I renounce and reject destructive cycles of shame, blame, fear, control, rebellion, and rejection. Cleanse my mind and replace negative thoughts with positive ones.

Father, in the name of Jesus Christ strengthen me to walk in my true identity as Your *beloved* son/daughter. I receive Your love, humility, presence, power, wisdom, and revelation. Fill me with the fruit of Your Spirit, including love, joy, peace, patience, kindness, goodness, gentleness, faithfulness, and self-control.[6]

In addition, if surgery is necessary, give me strength and confidence in You, and enable me to face this surgery with a peace that surpasses understanding.[7] Give my doctors, nurses, and all medical teams supernatural skill, wisdom, and discernment. I pray your protection over me before, during, and after surgery. I ask for quick healing and a full recovery.

Father, I am asking You to bless me, my spouse, my family and my entire generational line with great health. I ask all this in the mighty names of God, Holy Spirit, and Jesus Christ of Nazareth. Amen.

+ + +

Shock, Trauma, and Fear Prayer

As pastoral counselors who had previous careers as first responders—we know that shock, trauma, and fear are areas that people often minimize. The negative effects of traumatic events have consequences that are often difficult to quantify. Therefore, they are simply over-looked. We often lead individuals through a strategic prayer that we suggest be read aloud.

Lord Jesus, I ask by the power of the Holy Spirit that You remove all shock, trauma, and fear from:

> the cells of my body
>
> my organs
>
> my muscles, ligaments, tendons, joints, cartilage, bones, and bone marrow
>
> my blood stream and my DNA
>
> my nervous system—from the stem of my brain to my nerve endings.

I ask Lord Jesus that you pour Your healing oil into my nervous system:

> my mind on the conscious, subconscious, and unconscious level
>
> my emotions, my will, my spirit, and my identity
>
> all cognitive and verbal memories
>
> all non-cognitive and pre-verbal memories
>
> my amygdale
>
> my hypothalamus.

Please return them to their natural functioning states.

Turn off the alarm systems and the hyper-vigilance within me.

I ask Lord Jesus that You would receive all the silent screams from my body.

I ask that You would turn off the *fight and flight* response that has been activated by shock and trauma from events in my life.

Restore the *fight and flight* response to your original design within me.

I ask Lord Jesus that You would restore my brain to its natural homeostasis and that You would establish new neurological connections within me to the joy center. Lord Jesus, I ask that You would fill my cells with Your peace, Your love, Your joy. Please bring my body to a place of rest.

I ask all this in the name of Jesus. Amen.[8]

✦ ✦ ✦

Prayer to Break Viet Cong Curse

Viet Nam veterans report evidence that indicates a curse in the form of a ritualistic prayer was spoken over military personnel who were involved in combat in Viet Nam. The primary elements of the curse include: *you will be a wanderer, you will be filled with rage, and you will never have peace.* If you are a veteran and struggle with some of these issues, we encourage you to pray the following strategic prayer out loud.

Father God,

I acknowledge that I was involved in the Viet Nam war during my military service to my country.

I confess all sinful behavior associated with that war.

I ask You to forgive me for anything I did (knowingly or unknowingly) that could have connected me to this Viet Nam curse.

I receive Your forgiveness.

I forgive every officer who gave me an order to commit any sin.

I forgive everyone who encouraged me to enter into any sinful behavior rather than helping me deal with the stressful effects of war.

I forgive myself for any sinful behavior I engaged in during the war and after the war.

I will no longer hold myself guilty, because I know God has forgiven me.

I give all the stress, pain, anger, guilt, and shame to You, Lord, and I ask You to take it from me.

I want to leave it in the past and not carry it with me into the future.

I break the Viet Cong Curse that was spoken over me and every other military soldier.

I declare I am not a wanderer: that is a lie I no longer believe.

I declare I will no longer hold on to anger about anything associated with the war.

I declare I will no longer act out of rage because of my involvement in the war.

I declare that I have the peace of God in my life, and it guards my heart and my mind.[9]

This strategic prayer is focused on Viet Nam, but feel free to create your own prayer if you were involved in recent wars. Including: Gulf, Bosnian, Kosovo, Afghanistan, and Iraq wars; along with any military conflict.

Addiction Prayer

Addiction is a growing problem in our culture. In recent years, food addiction and eating disorders have resulted in many negative consequences. Interestingly, the very first temptation in the Garden of Eden included food. The serpent enticed the woman to eat the forbidden fruit, saying, "Did God really say, 'You must not eat from any tree in the garden'?"[10]

Following is a suggested prayer for anyone who struggles with food addiction. We encourage this prayer to be prayed out loud.

Thank You, Lord, for this new day!

Help me to recognize, resist, renounce, and reject addiction to food. Remove any strongholds of addiction from my life and generational line. Deepen my understanding of the spiritual dimension to food addiction and unhealthy eating.

I repent for:

Failing to honor the Holy Spirit who lives in me.[11]

Sins of overeating, gluttony, greed, excess, and selfishness.

Making my stomach my small-*g* god. Philippians 3:19 (NIV) says, "*Their destiny is destruction, their god is their stomach, and their glory is in their shame. Their mind is set on earthly things.*"

Idolatry of food, looking to it for comfort; expecting food to meet my deepest needs.

Addiction related specifically to sugar and bad carbs.

Not modeling healthy lifestyle choices to others.

Making unhealthy food choices that result in poor health.

Deliver me from food addiction.

Renew my mind[12] to not respond to food *triggers*.

Restore my body, mind, and soul to crave life-giving healthy foods.

Help me to stay humble and to live in the Larger Story.

Bless me with mental strength, godly discipline, great health, and wholeness.

I pray these prayers in the name of Jesus Christ of Nazareth.[13]

As your review these strategic prayers, feel free to modify them in order to address your specific needs. For example, in the addiction prayer, you may replace food with tobacco (nicotine), alcohol, marijuana, pain killers, prescription drugs, cocaine, heroin, benzodiazepines, opioids, stimulants, inhalants, or sedatives (barbiturates).

It's important to be aware that people also struggle with addictions that have become socially acceptable. For example, a person can be rewarded for being a workaholic. People can also become addicted to a lifestyle that idolizes financial gain, fame, and power; the next promotion; accumulating more; shopping; or even over-exercising. It is often much harder for people to identify these as addictions. But they are unhealthy lifestyles that block intimacy with God and can negatively impact one's relationship with a spouse and others.[14]

+ + +

Prayer for Humility

One strategic prayer we regularly pray relates to choosing *humility* over pride.[15] The Bible talks a lot about pride and humility. It is interesting to note that the Bible *never* frames pride in a positive light. On the other hand, it regularly frames humility in favorable ways. For example, James 4:6 says, "God is opposed to the proud, but gives grace to the humble." Matthew 23:12 says, "Whoever exalts himself shall be humbled; and whoever humbles himself shall be exalted."

Praying for humility is a wise prayer for a follower of Christ to pray. Humility opens the door to living in the Larger Story where *God* is the main character and *it's not about me*, instead of living in the smaller story where *you* are the main character and life *is all about me*. The following is a strategic prayer that focuses on rejecting pride and choosing humility. We encourage you to pray this out loud.

> Lord, Your Word says, "*You are opposed to the proud, but give grace to the humble.*"[16] And, "*Whoever exalts himself shall be humbled; and whoever humbles himself shall be exalted.*"[17]

> Father, clothe me with Your mantle of humility[18] and enable me to resist pride.

> When You ask me to do something, give me the strength to obey your commands, rather than doing life *my way*—or pridefully "striking the rock" like Moses did.[19]

Lord, today I choose to live in the Larger Story where *You* are the main character—and life is *not about me.*

+ + +

Spiritual Warfare Prayer

Life Is Lived in a Story

tim

Decades ago, I had a desire to pray in a more strategic way for our marriage and family. I had been reading books on spiritual warfare, healing, and deliverance. And I learned that prayer can be an offensive weapon that provides protection against the attacks of the enemy. So, I made the decision to more purposefully pray for my marriage and family in what I believed was a spiritual-warfare fashion. Over time, I developed the following prayer. It is a prayer that I continue to pray out loud pretty much every day.

> I declare to all powers and principalities and to all demons and enemy forces that God has given me the desire, ability, and authority to pray. Therefore, may nothing interfere with my prayer life for my marriage, family, friends, REAL LIFE ministries, and our *missionaries to marriage* calling.

> Lord, enable me to love, care for, honor, respect, and sacrifice for Anne, our kids, grandkids, and others. In the name of Jesus of Nazareth, I forbid the enemy and any evil spirits from attacking or scheming against my wife, children, grandchildren, friends, or me.

> In Jesus' name and truth and in the sacred blood of the Lamb, I specifically address every scheme of the enemy: You have no power, authority, or legal rights in my marriage, family, home, or ministry. Any and all schemes, curses, footholds, strongholds, generational sins, and iniquities are canceled and returned to the sender with blessings.

> Any ground previously gained by the evil one is taken back in the power of God the

Father, Holy Spirit, and in the name of Jesus Christ. Lord, please daily fill me, my wife, my children, my grandchildren, and future generations with Your Holy Spirit.

I humbly pray this prayer in the name, power, and authority of God the Father, God the Son, and God the Holy Spirit. I also pray this prayer in the authority You have given me as co-leader in my marriage and servant-leader in my family, home, and ministry.

We challenge you to write a spiritual warfare prayer of your own. People who implement these types of prayers tell us they are more aware of spiritual battles, they better understand the authority they have in Jesus name, and they experience the protection prayerfully engaging in spiritual warfare provides. And in marriages, our experience is when couples pray the above types of prayers, it helps them to walk in greater freedom—and *advance* in intimacy.

+ + +

Prayer for Marriage Reformation

One of the ways we describe the call on our lives is by saying we are *missionaries to marriage*. God has given us a desire to see people embrace and walk out His creational marriage design—one man and one woman co-leading—*together*.

Living that out in practical ways involves understanding the principles in Paradise such as mutuality, shared authority, and functional equality (co-leadership). From the beginning, God created the man and woman in His image—they were intrinsically equal. And they were both given the procreation and dominion mandates—they were functionally equal.[20]

Following is a strategic prayer that focuses on Marriage Reformation. We encourage you to pray this out loud.

God, empower my spouse and I to passionately live out Your creational marriage design as we supernaturally reclaim what's been stolen. Lord, protect and enable us to experience marriage transformation that ignites Marriage Reformation.

+ + +

Prayer for Family Protection

Recently, we came across a prayer in a *Ransomed Heart* newsletter that we immediately added to our regular prayers. It involves declaring God's love over those we love.

> I bring the Love of God the Father, the Love of Jesus Christ, the Love of the Holy Spirit over my heart and over my life today, over my home and family (name them), over my household and domain. I command the Love of God to fill and shield my household and domain. I command the Love of God against all Hatred set against us—Love as our shield against Hatred in this hour. I command this in the name of Jesus Christ.[21]

+ + +

Prayer for the Holy Spirit

The Godhead includes the Father, Son, and Spirit. Often people admit to relating more closely to one of the three persons in the Trinity. We have heard people say they identify with God as Father, or Jesus Christ as the Son of God—their Savior. But often people have questions related to the life and ministry of the Holy Spirit.

Isaiah 11:2–3 describes some of the Holy Spirit's ministry. Including: "The *Spirit of the Lord* will rest on Him, the spirit of *wisdom* and of *understanding*, the spirit of *counsel* and of *might*, the spirit of the *knowledge* and *fear of the Lord*. And he will delight in the fear of the Lord." In addition, the fruit of the Holy Spirit includes l*ove, joy, peace, patience, kindness, goodness, gentleness, faithfulness, and self-control.*[22]

Some people consider the filling of the Holy Spirit as a one-time event. Others view it as a continual supernatural filling that is available to every follower of Christ who asks. Therefore, because the Holy Spirit is so important in every believer's life and marriage, we would like to share a strategic prayer that can be prayed daily. It's based on a song written by Rory Nolan. We encourage you to pray this prayer out loud.

Holy Spirit take control,

take my body, mind, and soul,

put a finger on anything I do that grieves you,

anything that doesn't please you,

Holy Spirit take control.[23]

REAL LIFE Questions

1. What observations can you make about praying strategically?

_____

_____

2. The Bible says, "You do not have because you do not ask God."[24] What specific prayer(s) in this chapter have you been encouraged to pray?

_____

_____

3. What is one specific request would you like to make to God regarding your marriage?

_____

_____

4. Review Prayer for the Holy Spirit.

Are you filled with the Holy Spirit? Yes_____ No_____ Briefly explain.

_____

_____

If No, would you be willing to ask God to fill you with the Holy Spirit? Yes_____ No_____

_____

_____

Is your spouse filled with the Holy Spirit? Yes_____ No_____ Briefly explain.

_____

_____

If No, do you think they would they be willing to ask God to fill them with the Holy Spirit?
Yes_____ No_____ Briefly explain.

_____

_____

REAL LIFE Couples Application

As a couple, write out a spiritual warfare prayer of your own. Pray it consistently (daily) for two weeks. Then *together* review how praying this prayer impacted you and your marriage. Journal your thoughts.

_____

_____

_____

_____

Listening to God—I.O.T.L. (*Inquire of the Lord*)

Inviting God into your day by including Him, even in the little things, is one way to build intimacy with Him. Hebrews 12:25 says, "See to it that you do not refuse Him who is speaking." In other words, God *is* speaking, but are you taking the time to listen? At the end of each chapter, we include a *Listening to God* section. This provides an opportunity to *Inquire of the Lord* (I.O.T.L.) and ask the following questions:

+ *Lord, is there anything You want to highlight for me in this section?*

_____

_____

+ *Is there a specific step You want me to take?*

_____

_____

+ *Is there anything You would like me to share with my spouse?*

_____

_____

+ Journal anything you sense the Lord may be saying to you.

_____

_____

CHAPTER 12

DEVELOPING A PRAYER SHIELD

When we worked at the World Prayer Center for Global Harvest Ministries in Colorado Springs, our prayer life took a giant step forward. *Why?* Because we were surrounded by people who were passionate about prayer. The ways they modeled prayer not only served to mentor us, but also transformed the ways we related to God. During that season of our lives, we were also introduced to Dr. C. Peter Wagner's book series on prayer.

Our favorite book in that series was titled: *Prayer Shield*.[1] In his book, Dr. Wagner described a prayer shield team as any number of people who are intentional about their commitment to pray for an individual, family, church, ministry, organization, or nation.

Life Is Lived in a Story

tim

When I look back over my life, prayer has been a common thread. As a child, I grew up in a home with a praying mom. She wasn't someone who talked a lot about her faith or prayer life. There was nothing religious about her. My mom's simple faith motivated her to respond to life with prayer. And all five of her children grew up knowing they were the focus of her prayers. As I review growing up, I see that my mom was a consistent prayer shield for me and our family.

As I got older, God brought a man into my life who became our first small group leader. His name was Dick Swetman. It didn't take me long to figure out that Dick was a *list-prayer*. He also prayed Scriptures over the people on his list. When you were on his *list*, you knew you were being prayed for on a daily basis. Since Dick was such an important part of our daily life, we regularly updated him on our family's prayer needs. Almost every time we were together, or just talking on the phone, he would remind me that he loved me and was praying for me.

Dick was the first man in my life to model a faithful and disciplined prayer life. He mentored me over the years by the way he lived rather than by what he said. He daily prayed on his knees for our marriage and family for over thirty years. And he taught me what it meant to ask, seek, and knock, "Ask, and it will be given to you; seek, and you will find; knock, and it will be opened to you."[2]

Dick went home to be with the Lord over ten years ago. I will never fully understand, this side of heaven, the countless ways his prayers protected our family. For decades he was a part of our prayer shield before we even knew what having a prayer shield meant.

+ + +

Dr. Wagner's *Prayer Shield* book motivated us to create a prayer shield team. Over the years, we had always been surrounded by a few faithful people who prayed for us, our marriage, our family, and our ministry. But as we sensed God inviting us to develop a prayer shield team, we asked people who were already praying if they would be willing to commit to strategically praying for us on a regular basis.

Over the years, our small group of faithful intercessors has kept increasing. When we travel, lead workshops, or speak at churches, we invite people to *Inquire of the Lord* (**I.O.T.L.**) and consider signing up to be part of our prayer shield team. As the team grew, we decided to send out regular newsletters to update the prayer shield team members with current prayer requests. We also have a smaller prayer shield team of intercessors committed to praying for private family needs and requests.

We are so serious about the importance of having a prayer shield that whenever we go to local churches to minister, we have two non-negotiable requirements.

1 - First, the authority of church leadership is extended to us.
2 - Second, a prayer shield team is in place before, during, and after each REAL LIFE marriage gathering.

Having a prayer shield team in place provides protection. It reminds us that *God is God—and we're not!* In our experience, a focused prayer shield team provides supernatural power and protection. We resonate with Mother Theresa's quote, "There is a tremendous strength that is growing in the world through sharing together, praying together, suffering together, and working together."[3]

REAL LIFE Questions

1. Make some observations about the benefits of a prayer shield team.

_____

_____

2. Who are the people in your life that you identify as *pray-ers (intercessors)*. List them below.

_____

_____

3. Would you consider asking these people to commit to praying for you and your family on a regular basis?   Yes_____   No_____

If yes, what steps would you take to keep them updated on your prayer needs? If No, briefly explain.

_____

_____

_____

4. What steps are you willing to take in order to have a more consistent prayer life?

_____

_____

REAL LIFE Couples Application

Discuss with your spouse the benefits in developing a strategic *prayer shield* specifically for your marriage. What might that look like?

_____

_____

_____

Who would you invite to be a part of your *marriage prayer shield*?

_____

_____

What specific next steps do you agree to take?

_____

_____

Schedule a time/date and together review your answers to the above questions.

_____

_____

Listening to God—I.O.T.L. (*Inquire of the Lord*).

Inviting God into your day by including Him, even in the little things, is one way to build intimacy with Him. Hebrews 12:25 says, "See to it that you do not refuse Him who is speaking." In other words, God *is* speaking, but are you taking the time to listen? At the end of each chapter, we include a *Listening to God* section. This provides an opportunity to *Inquire of the Lord* (I.O.T.L.) by encouraging you to practice asking these questions:

+ *Lord, is there anything You want to highlight for me in this section?*

_____

_____

+ *Is there a specific step You want me to take?*

_____

_____

+ *Is there anything You would like me to share with my spouse?*

_____

_____

+ Journal anything you sense the Lord may be saying to you.

_____

_____

CHAPTER 13

THE PRACTICE OF SURRENDER

Life Is Lived in a Story

anne

Tim and I have always enjoyed walking outside together. When our children were younger, we began to turn our evening walks into opportunities to pray together. After dinner, walking was a good way for the kids to get outside. We pushed them in strollers or wagons. As they got older, we'd walk behind them praying while they rode their bikes ahead of us. It was so natural that the kids never knew we were prayer walking; they just thought we were all heading to the park—and we were!

For us, prayer walking continued long after our children left our home. And now that we live in Colorado, the mountains have transformed our *walking* into *hiking* experiences that have resulted in many sweet moments with God. Often after a long day, we'll grab our hiking boots and drive to a nearby trailhead. A favorite of ours is Red Rock Canyon Open Space. I can't tell you how many *world problems* we've solved on those trails!

In addition to hiking, another interest we have is reading. Tim regularly reminds our grandchildren that "leaders are readers." We also love to learn new things. I might even describe us as full-time students of life. We love to process God's truths together and look for ways to apply them in our lives and marriage. I recall one particular season when I felt like everything I was hearing, reading, and personally experiencing was challenging me to *live in the present moment*. Rather than being distracted with regrets (from the *past*) or anxiety (about the *future*), God was encouraging me to live in the *present—the now*.

I remember my heart resonated with that challenge. I wanted to learn more about what it meant to fully celebrate each moment as if it were my last. I want to be a person who is able to let go of things that block me from *advancing* in intimacy with God, Tim, and others. And just like anything I want to get better at, I knew it would take practice. As an aside, I have always been a visual and auditory learner. So, whenever I am learning new things, I always look for ways to *see* it and *hear* it so I can understand it better.

During this particular season, God was inviting me to connect with Him in deeper ways by living in the present moment. Over a period of time, I was *practicing* what I was learning and challenging myself to purposefully walk it out. I remember being excited to share what I was learning with Tim. But I wanted to wait for the right time. After all, I didn't want to just *tell* him what I was learning; I wanted to *show* him, so we could *practice* it—*together*.

I can still remember the day Tim and I drove to Red Rock Canyon to hike. I suggested we take a specific trail that begins in a large open space before heading into the mountains. It's one of my favorite settings. The land slopes down from the trail creating an enormous shallow bowl while Pikes Peak frames the backside of the valley.

About a mile into the hike my heart rate was beginning to increase. As we reached the top of the open space, we stopped for a moment. I asked Tim if he was up for *practicing* some of the things God was teaching me. Not quite sure where I was going, he reluctantly agreed. I warned him that this exercise would require some imagination. Because I am a visual learner, Tim is rarely surprised by my word pictures.

Every year on Labor Day in Colorado Springs, Tim and I attend the Hot Air Balloon Festival. Since the balloons launch early, Tim has always lured me out of bed before sunrise with the promise of a cup of hot coffee from Dunkin' Donuts. Once I have some coffee in my hands, we drive around the perimeter of Memorial Park watching a sea of colorful hot air balloons getting ready to launch. If you are driving anywhere near I-25 that morning, you will see a spectacular parade of colorful balloons floating along the Front Range.

I began by reminding Tim of our Labor Day tradition and then asked him to "take a few cleansing breaths. And then imagine one of those colorful hot air balloons anchored in the center of the valley before us." He nodded as he began to describe in detail the balloon he was imagining.

I continued, "In your mind's eye, look into the basket of the balloon, and imagine the Lord is the pilot. He's inviting you to unpack all your burdens, disappointments, discouragement, doubts, and unfilled dreams—and hand them to Him. As you give Jesus all the things you no longer want to carry, imagine Him placing those things inside the basket of the hot air balloon."

As an aside: This is just one part of Tim I love. Even after forty plus years of marriage, he is more than willing to give something a try—especially when it comes to *advancing* in intimacy with God and others. I continued encouraging him by saying, "Keep your eyes closed, continue to take cleansing breaths, inhale God's peace, and exhale all the stress you are carrying. As you focus on listening to the Lord, ask Him to show you if there is anything else He wants you to give Him."

Tim spoke aloud, "Father, is there anything You would like me to give to You? Are there any negative emotions—unrighteous anger—stress—fears—unforgiveness—or unrighteous judgment that I'm holding on to?"

We stood in silence for what seemed like a long time, but it was probably only a matter of minutes. I prayed for Tim as he continued to walk through the exercise. Tim explained what the Lord was bringing to mind and shared some things that he said he had not thought about in a while. When I asked him if he was willing to surrender those things, he said *yes*. I suggested he imagine symbolically handing each one to the Lord.

After surrendering them to the Lord, I asked him to imagine the balloon lifting off the ground. We stood together quietly, gazing at the sky as we were visualizing the imaginary balloon disappearing into the heavens. It was so peaceful, quiet, life-giving.

Tim looked at me and smiled. Without saying a word, we continued hiking down the trail. After a mile or so, he shared how much lighter he felt. On a personal note: Whenever I symbolically *let go* of something and give it to the Lord, I always ask God to replace it. For example, in place of unforgiveness, I *receive* forgiveness. In place of unbelief, I *receive* increased faith. Instead of hopelessness, I *receive* renewed hope. In place of anxiety and fear, I *receive* peace and courage.

I am learning that in order to live in the present and celebrate the now moment—I need to *let go* and *surrender* the things that keep me distracted and then ask God to replace those things. Rather than living with the consequences of unrighteous anger, regret, or anxiety, I can position myself to be still and focus on God.[1] Rather than being weighed down with un-forgiveness or unfulfilled dreams, I can choose to surrender and ask God to fill those places with good things. Tim and I regularly repeat this hot air balloon prayer of surrender. We refer to it as our *mind-cleansing exercise*.

REAL LIFE Questions

1. Make some observations about your ability to live in the present moment. Briefly explain.

_____

_____

What observations do you think your spouse would make about your ability to let go, surrender, live in the moment? Briefly explain.

_____

_____

2. What specific steps are you willing to take to enjoy more present moments with God, yourself, your spouse, and others?

_____

_____

3. How would taking those specific steps positively impact your life, your relationship with God, your spouse, and your family?

_____

_____

4. In the hot air balloon story, when a person symbolically lets go of something and gives it to the Lord, it's not only important to ask God to replace it with something, but also to make sure you receive it. For example, in place of anxiety and stress, I _receive_ peace. In place of negative self-talk, I _receive_ my true, God-given identity as a _beloved_ son/daughter. Write down something you would like to symbolically give to the Lord. Next, write down what you would like God to give you in place of what you let go of.

_____

_____

REAL LIFE Couples Application

Review Anne's mind-cleanse story. As a couple, invite the Holy Spirit to lead you in a mind-cleanse surrender. You can use the hot air balloon example or create your own scenario. Remember when you let go of something and surrender it to the Lord, ask Him to refill that place in your heart. We challenge the husband to lead out one time and the wife to lead out another time.

_____

_____

_____

Schedule a time/date and together review how your mind-cleanse surrender exercise played out.

_____

_____

_____

Listening to God—I.O.T.L. (*Inquire of the Lord*)

Inviting God into your day by including Him, even in the little things, is one way to build intimacy with Him. Hebrews 12:25 says, "See to it that you do not refuse Him who is speaking." In other words, God *is* speaking, but are you taking the time to listen? At the end of each chapter, we include a *Listening to God* section. This provides an opportunity to *Inquire of the Lord* (I.O.T.L.) and ask the following questions:

+ *Lord, is there anything You want to highlight for me in this section?*

_____

+ *Is there a specific step You want me to take?*

_____

+ Is there anything You would like me to share with my spouse?

_____

+ Journal anything you sense the Lord may be saying to you.

_____

_____

CHAPTER 14

HUSBANDS ARE YOUR PRAYERS HINDERED?

Life Is Lived in a Story

tim

If you are a husband who has a strong desire to grow in deeper intimacy with your spouse, then you are in the right chapter. As a retired fireman, I've always liked a good challenge. So, if you're anything like me, you'll want to explore a passage in 1 Peter and see what the Bible says about how a husband should treat his wife.

> You husbands in the same way, live with your wives in an understanding way, as with someone weaker, since she is a woman; and show her honor as a fellow heir of the grace of life, so that your prayers will not be hindered.[1]

In the Same Way

To begin, when the Bible says *in the same way*, it is important to revisit the previous passages. *In the same way* in 1 Peter 3:1 relates to the previous passages in chapter 2 that talk about following Jesus Christ's example: "For you have been called for this purpose, since Christ also suffered for you, leaving you an example for you to follow in His steps...while being reviled, He did not revile in return; while suffering, He uttered no threats, but kept entrusting *Himself* to Him who judges righteously."[2]

Accordingly, wives are to model, *in the same ways*, Jesus' behaviors. This includes following His example, and when you are reviled—which means "to criticize in an abusive or angrily insulting manner"[3]—do not revile in return. And when you suffer, utter no threats. Instead, keep entrusting yourself to God who judges righteously.

Next, husbands are addressed: You husbands *in the same way*.[4] This command connects to the preceding passages that addressed wives. Accordingly, husbands are to behave *in the same ways* as wives. And this includes focusing on the "hidden person of the heart, with the imperishable quality of a gentle and quiet spirit."[5] As an aside, Jesus only described Himself one time in the Bible—in Matthew 11:29—where He said, "I am gentle and humble in heart." Husbands, would your wife, or people who know you well, describe you as *gentle and humble in heart?*

After wives are told to behave *in the same ways* as Jesus, and husbands are told to behave *in the same way* as wives, husbands are specifically challenged to "live with your wives in an understanding way, as with someone weaker, since she is a woman; and show her honor as a fellow heir of the grace of life, so that your prayers will not be hindered."[6]

It's important to note that when this passage says, *as with someone weaker,* it does not mean that a husband has superior emotional or spiritual strength. Figuratively speaking, a husband could be described as a milk pitcher and a wife described as a priceless vase. Both containers can be used to hold liquids. However, they are valuable in different ways. Also, it's important to note that the word *weaker* does not refer to a hierarchal or patriarchal relationship where a husband has authority over his wife.

Understanding Your Spouse

When I read the command, "Live with your wives in an *understanding way,*"[7] I am thankful that this passage does not command, *understand your spouse.* Personally, I do not think it's possible to *totally understand* a spouse. Instead, the text says to live with a spouse i*n an understanding way*, which I believe is possible.

Husbands, I realize that trying to live with your wife in an *understanding way* is a *big* command. And I'm not asking you to do anything I'm not personally challenged to do in my own life. I'm writing from the perspective of being married for decades. And the reality is, even after forty-three years of marriage, I will never totally understand my bride. *Why?* Because she is a woman, and I am a man. And even though we are intrinsically equal, functionally equal, and are similar in many ways—we are also very different.

That said, although I will never *totally understand* Anne, I am committed to never stop trying to understand her. Just as my good Father continues to pursue me, to the best of my ability I will continue to pursue my bride—*in good times and bad, in sickness and health*.

For anyone who is serious about growing in marriage, 1 Peter 3 is a passage you will want to study. In fact, I encourage both husbands and wives who want to keep advancing in intimacy with God and their spouse to spend time investing in Bible study. It's also important to be in community. This includes having godly people in your life who love, support, encourage, pray for—and challenge you.

Regarding challenges, I challenge every husband to invite close friends to give you feedback. Specifically, ask them to share any observations they have about the ways you treat your wife. Do they see you living with her in an *understanding way*? Do they observe you to be a man who honors and respects your wife? Remember, love, honor, and respect go hand in hand. Being open to receiving feedback from godly men is a practical way to provide accountability in your life. As you are transparent, teachable, and make yourself available to mentors, you will better see any blind spots you may have.

This book's main focus is prayer, and the 1 Peter passage makes an amazing connection between a husband's behaviors toward his wife and prayer. It says when a husband lives in an *understanding way* and *honors* a spouse—*his prayers will not be hindered*.[8]

I frequently talk with husbands who feel stuck in their prayer life. They describe feeling as if their prayers are weak, blocked, or hindered. As the Holy Spirit leads, I share the 1 Peter passage with them. Then I look them in the eyes and say, "Of course I can't speak for God. And I don't know why some prayers feel like they are hindered and other prayers don't. But as a man made in God's image, I can make the volitional choice to take ownership and responsibility for my choices. And 1 Peter says the way I treat my wife is directly connected to my prayer life. In other words, all I can do is my part. Therefore, I can make every effort to live with my wife in an understanding way and intentionally look for ways to honor her."

More times than not, after I share this passage, husbands are encouraged to be more intentional about the ways they treat their wives. And they are challenged to take ownership and responsibility for the part of their marriage relationship they can control.

All that is to say, I offer every husband a personal challenge: *Will you commit to living out the truths in this passage? For three months, will you purposefully live in an understanding way and honor your bride?* As you do this, observe how your prayer life—and marriage—are impacted.

+ + +

Life Is Lived in a Story

anne

As I read Tim's challenge to husbands, I'd like to give my own perspective. For me, 1 Peter 3:7 has been a very powerful Scripture. And the longer we are together, the more we view marriage as an opportunity to reflect and reveal God to each other.

For example, early in our marriage, as we were just beginning to relate to God in new and deeper ways, I would hear messages about how God loved me and has never stopped pursuing me. As encouraging as that was for me to hear, it wasn't the kind of relationship I had personally experienced with God. So, I simply stored that away in my "good to know" file.

And then one day, I had a wake-up call. I realized that Tim's pursuit of me—especially as he tried to better understand and honor me—reflected some of the ways that God feels about me. My husband's attempts to live with me in an understanding way and honor me encouraged me to more fully trust God.

I remember thinking to myself, *If this is what it feels like to be loved and honored by Tim—how much more God loves and honors me. And if this is what it feels like to be forgiven by Tim—how much greater God's forgiveness is.* Making that connection allowed me to *receive* the truth of God's Word—and *believe* it in my heart. And even after forty-three years of marriage, God continues to invite me to trust Him more, and He uses my growing trust in Tim as a model that both encourages and challenges me.

+ + +

As I (tim) reflect back over the years, after processing this 1 Peter text with husbands, often an insightful question emerges. They ask, "When did a man not live with his wife in an understanding way and fail to show her honor as a fellow heir of the grace of life? When did the mistreatment of women begin?" That's a great question, one Anne and I have thought about for some time. My response is to remind husbands that headship, hierarchy, patriarchy, the mistreatment of women, the idea of the man being designated as the wife's leader, and the idea of spiritual covering were not present in God's original design for marriage—before sin entered the story.

In addition, our counseling experiences suggest that there is a wide range that husbands fall into regarding how they invest in living with their wives in an *understanding way* and showing them *honor* as fellow heirs of the grace of life. Unfortunately, living as reciprocal servants in mutuality and functional equality is *not* the typical default for most men.

That said, in addition to *understanding and honoring* a wife, another Bible text, says, "*Submit to one another* out of reverence for Christ."[9] This passage clearly commands *mutual submission* in all relationships, and that includes marriage.

Ephesians 5:25 (NIV) says, "Husbands, *love your wives*, just as Christ loved the church and gave himself up for her." Jesus loved and died for the church; likewise, husbands should be willing to love and die for their spouse. Verse 28 (NIV) says, "*In this same way*, husbands ought to love their wives as their own bodies. He who loves his wife loves himself." My takeaway from that passage is a husband who lives out biblical headship[10] has a healthy self-love, and this becomes the pathway to more whole-heartedly loving, honoring, treasuring—and being willing to die for his bride.

When I have conversations about marriage with husbands, often the subject of *authority* comes up. Many husbands believe they have authority over their spouse. When they make that claim, I ask them to explain their perspective surrounding the passage in 1 Corinthians that specifically addresses authority in marriage. It says, "The wife does not have authority over her own body, but the husband *does*; and likewise also the husband does not have authority over his own body, but the wife *does*."[11] This passage clearly commands *mutual authority* in marriage.

Most men I share the above passages with (1 Peter 3:7; Ephesians 5:21; 1 Corinthians 7:4) are eager to commit to better *understanding, honoring, treasuring, being willing to die for*, and unconditionally *loving* their spouse. Unfortunately, there are other men who refuse to treat their wives as fellow/joint heirs who are functional equals. They tend to default to hierarchy, patriarchy, complementarianism, forced female subordination, and unbiblical forms of headship. On the extreme end of the continuum are men who abuse wives. And these behaviors are accompanied with all sorts of painful and negative consequences that result in a husband's *prayers being hindered*.[12]

This book is on prayer, and in this chapter we've shared a number of passages surrounding how a husband should treat his wife. That said, we want to *briefly* address husbands abusing wives. While abuse has been going on for centuries, thankfully in recent years it has gotten enormous amounts of attention. Do you ever wonder *why* abuse is so rampant?

After working with many women who have experienced abuse, we wonder, *Might the root of abuse involve misogyny—which means "dislike of, contempt for, or ingrained prejudice against women."*[13] Men who display a misogynistic bent consciously or subconsciously, actively or passively, often struggle with contempt for and a deep-seated hatred toward women. *Any* form of abuse is diametrically opposed to the commands for husbands to *live with your wife in an understanding way, show her honor as a fellow heir of the grace of life,*[14] and *submit to one another out of reverence for Christ.*[15]

Returning to the above question, we believe the mistreatment of women began after the Fall. We believe misogyny—*dislike of, contempt for, or ingrained prejudice against women*—came after sin entered the story and the woman became subject to the man. Review the text. One of the first consequences of sin was that God said to the woman, "Your desire will be for your husband, and *he will rule over you.*"[16] Sadly, many husbands cowardly leverage a wife's unhealthy, co-dependent, or dysfunctional desire for them, and they default to male rulership or toxic complementarian positions. And this can lead some husbands to attempt to control, rule over, dominate, and—in more severe cases—abuse a wife.

Throughout the years, we have made a list of misogynistic tendencies and behaviors, including: *male rulership, hierarchical and patriarchal abuses, forced female subordination, headship abuses, unbiblical complementarian abuses, a misogynistic women-hating spirit, spiritual abuse, emotional abuse, sexual abuse, mental abuse, physical abuse, verbal abuse, and toxic leadership abuse.*

Our primary desire in writing this book is to not just to talk about prayer—but to teach readers to pray.[17] One way to do that is to offer a number of strategic prayers. Concerning abuse, if you have experienced any form of it, we encourage you to pray the following prayer out loud.

> *In the name that is above every name—Jesus Christ, I renounce and reject: male rulership, hierarchical and patriarchal abuses, forced female subordination, headship abuses, unbiblical complementarian abuses, a misogynistic women-hating spirit, spiritual abuse, emotional abuse, sexual abuse, mental abuse, physical abuse, verbal abuse, and toxic leadership abuse. I recognize, renounce, and reject any ways these behaviors negatively impacted me—my heart, body, mind, soul, marriage, and relationships.*

Additionally, if the abuse is ongoing, get to a safe environment. If necessary, contact the proper authorities. Maintain healthy boundaries and develop a *team* to walk with you. As an aside, we are working on a book titled *ABUSE: Experiencing Freedom through Forgiveness,* which will be available soon.

Returning to the 1 Peter text, after first addressing wives and then husbands, it addresses *all* men, women, husbands, and wives, saying, "Finally, *all of you*, be like-minded, be sympathetic, love one another, be compassionate and humble. Do not repay evil with evil or insult with insult. On the contrary, repay evil with blessing, because to this you were called so that you may inherit a blessing."[18] One of our spiritual mentors used to paraphrase the passage about not returning evil for evil or insult for insult. He would say, "*In our culture that emphasizes how important it is to look out for #1, remember that it is better to be the one stolen from than the one doing the stealing.*"

The end of verse 9 says to "repay evil with blessing." *Why?* "Because to this [blessing] you were called." Pause for a moment and consider what your life, marriage, churches, communities, and our culture would look like if followers of Christ focused on blessing others. We believe the transformation would be monumental and result in advancing God's Kingdom in dramatic ways.

REAL LIFE Questions

1. Husbands, as you read through 1 Peter 3:7, what specific applications can you make in your marriage that will have a positive impact on your prayer life?

_____

_____

2. Who are the men in your life who are godly role models for living out 1 Peter 3:7? List their names.

_____

_____

3. Are you willing to invite some of these men to give you honest feedback with regards to 1 Peter 3:7 Yes _____ No _____

If yes, what feedback did they give you?

_____

_____

What was your response to their feedback?

_____

_____

If you are unwilling to invite honest feedback, or you do not have any godly men you feel comfortable asking, what next steps are you willing to take in order to advance in better understanding and living out 1 Peter 3:7?

_____

_____

_____

4. This chapter asked an interesting question, When did a man not live with his wife in an understanding way and show her honor as a fellow heir of the grace of life? When did that originate? How would you answer that question?

_____

_____

5. Men, are you up for a real life challenge? Without telling your wife, invest thirty days purposefully focusing on honoring your bride and living with her in an understanding way. After thirty days, make some observations related to your:

Prayer life

_____

_____

Intimacy with your wife

_____

_____

REAL LIFE Questions for Wives:

1. Wives, as you read through 1 Peter 3:7, what specific applications can you make in your marriage?

_____

_____

2. In what ways do you help your husband to better understand and honor you?

_____

_____

_____

REAL LIFE Couples Application

Husbands, after completing this chapter, make some observations about how your relationship with your wife impacts your prayer life. Journal your thoughts and share them with your spouse.

_____

_____

_____

Wives, after completing this chapter, consider committing to pray for your husband and his relationship with the Lord. Ask your good Father for the desires of your heart related to your marriage relationship. Note: let the Holy Spirit be the One who counsels and convicts your husband—while you commit to pray for him. Journal your thoughts.

_____

_____

_____

Listening to God—I.O.T.L. (*Inquire of the Lord*)

Inviting God into your day by including Him, even in the little things, is one way to build intimacy with Him. Hebrews 12:25 says, "See to it that you do not refuse Him who is speaking." In other words, God *is* speaking, but are you taking the time to listen? At the end of each chapter, we include a *Listening to God* section. This provides an opportunity to *Inquire of the Lord* (**I.O.T.L.**) and ask the following questions:

+ *Lord, is there anything You want to highlight for me in this section?*

_____

+ *Is there a specific step You want me to take?*

_____

+ *Is there anything You would like me to share with my spouse?*

_____

+ Journal anything you sense the Lord may be saying to you.

_____

_____

CHAPTER 15

PRAYING TOGETHER

The Bible says, "Two are better than one, because they have a good return for their labor."[1] When you consider the strength that comes in numbers, praying is definitely on that list. For husbands and wives, certainly, prayer is a powerful connection with God, and the power increases when you pray with your spouse.

We regularly talk to couples who want to see God strengthen their marriage. Often, they share a sincere desire to advance in their prayer life—*together*. When we ask, "What do you think is blocking you from taking the next step," their response is often, "We've never really found a successful way to pray together that works for us. We are so different in the way we relate to God."

A Praying Marriage

Praying together is an invitation to engage with a good Father who unconditionally loves you and your spouse. Praying together helps a couple to connect with each other and to *advance* spiritually as well as emotionally. Couples who pray together realize it is much more than a spiritual discipline; it's an intimacy building experience.

But *advancing* in intimacy doesn't happen overnight or by accident. Meaningful relationships require time and intention. That said, a husband and wife pray not because they *have* to, but because they *get* to. Over time, as a couple prays together, they discover that drawing near to God results in drawing closer to each other.

Living in a stressful, noisy world can be exhausting. One of the negative impacts of a fast-paced lifestyle is it can become distracting. It pushes opportunities for intimacy and connection further down on the priority list. People have less and less time to connect with each other—let alone connect with God. Spiritual practices become something a couple only has time to read about. Each day is so full of activity that it's difficult to stay focused. We are living in a world where more and more people are experiencing symptoms of anxiety on a daily basis. And we believe this directly relates to the fast pace of life.

Constant noise negatively impacts a person's ability to hear God's still, soft voice. Thomas Merton said this: "The greatest need of our time is to clean out the enormous mass of mental and emotional rubbish that clutters our minds."[2]

In other words, if you desire to *advance* in intimacy with God and your spouse, it's going to require some changes to your life. Changes that create room to be still and embrace the sacred in silence as you *advance* in developing your listening skills.

In marriage, conversation between a husband and wife who are good listeners can feel as natural as breathing. Talking with God (*prayer*) is much the same. The progressive nature of intimacy increases your desire to invite God into every part of your life, marriage, family, friendships, ministry, and workplace. Relating with God in prayer is a life-giving source that rejuvenates your spirit—and marriage.

Prayer is simply turning your focus toward the One who is listening, the One who has the power to intervene, the One who can transform a heart, change a circumstance, or simply comfort a person who is hurting.

In marriage, prayer builds up a couple's faith. Hebrews 11:1 (NIV) says, "...Faith is confidence in what we hope for and assurance about what we do not see." When couples pray, they receive seeds of *hope* from the One who promises to listen, forgive, and restore. Similar to other spiritual disciplines, it has been our experience that a praying marriage leads to *advancing* in spirit + soul + body oneness, causing couples to enjoy more frequent SOUL*gasms* and truly experience what we often describe as a BEST MARRIAGE NOW.

+ + +

Life Is Lived in a Story

tim

When the two of us first started praying together, we often found the experience disappointing and at times frustrating. The truth was that we both related to God in very different ways. So, having a simple conversation with God—*together*—sounded challenging. I tended to become distracted when Anne was praying. Although I started out determined to listen, my mind would start to wander, and I became preoccupied with my own thoughts. Other times when Anne prayed, I got bored with what seemed to be her monologue to God. I felt as if I was listening in on someone else's private conversation. Instead of being a *participant* in a shared activity, I felt more like an *observer* as I listened to Anne praying.

In spite of the rough start, we were committed to *the practice* of praying together as a couple. We knew there was untapped power in a marriage that purposefully included prayer. We just had to figure out a way to make it more relevant—and enjoyable. One thing we didn't want to do was turn it into a routine, regimented religious activity. Prayer is supposed to model and celebrate a living *relationship* with a good Father, not a *duty* we're required to fulfill.

So, we decided to pray together by taking turns praying in short sentences. Going back and forth created a rhythm that we both participated in, and it kept our prayers flowing. It went something like this.

> Tim: "*Lord, we are thankful that You are good—and so good to us...*"
> Anne: "*Father, we are grateful for Your love and friendship...*"
> Tim: "*We praise You today for being such an amazing and loving God!*"
> Anne: "*Our time together with You today comes from hearts of worship...*"

We continue going back and forth until one of us shifts the prayer focus to another topic. For example, at some point we pray for our marriage and for each of our children and grandchildren by name.

> Anne: "Lord, thank for marriage, for Tim, for his integrity and character."
> Tim: "Lord, I agree—thank you for our marriage, for Anne, for her heart, her compas-

sion, and her passion to always be learning new things ..."

Anne: "Teach us what it means to leave a spiritual and marriage legacy to our kids, grandkids, and future generations..."

Tim: "Give us spirit + soul + body oneness and a very, very long, healthy, faithful, fruitful, and joyful marriage..."

Implementing this simple model of short one-sentence prayers revolutionized our prayer life. Praying short sentences allowed us to stay focused. Plus, it left room for many creative options. For example, sometimes we rotated through specific topics, like this:

Monday—people who don't know Jesus; outreach prayers...

Tuesday—marriage; family; extended family specific needs and desires...

Wednesday—friends, neighbors, school teachers, faculty, students, and co-workers...

Thursday—people who are sick, hurting, struggling...

Friday—the church, para-church, and local, national, world leaders...

Saturday—military, first responders, fire fighters, police...

Sunday—on this day we don't have an agenda or specific prayer focus. We listen to God and pray as the Spirit leads.

We encourage you to invite God into your process (**I.O.T.L.**) and ask the Lord for creative ways to pray. And then practice so you can discover what works best for you. There are unlimited *advancing* in intimacy possibilities in praying together. The Bible says, "If two of you agree here on earth concerning anything you ask, my Father in heaven will do it for you. For where two or three gather together as my followers, I am there among them."[3]

In our experience, when husbands and wives purposefully pray together, the enemy is not happy. This is one reason why praying together as a couple can be a struggle. The enemy will do anything he can to discourage you and your spouse from growing in this spiritual discipline. But be encouraged: "Greater is He who is in you, than he who is in the world."[4] There is untapped Kingdom of God and intimacy-*advancing* potential when a husband and wife encounter God through focused prayer.

Just as advancing in communication requires that a couple grow in their listening skills, so it is with prayer. Praying together includes learning to listen to the Holy Spirit—the One who strengthens, encourages, comforts, and provides power, protection, wisdom, and revelation. We are convinced that praying together strengthens a couple's oneness and leads to *advancing* in intimacy and more frequent SOUL*gasm* experiences. Following are some suggestions to help you pray together:

+ **I.O.T.L.** as you invite the Holy Spirit to lead your prayer times—and then listen.
+ Alternate back and forth, and reflect back and forth, to stay focused and hold your attention.
+ Use short, one-sentence prayers. Long monologues invite distractions.
+ Keep your prayers conversational. Remember prayer is about *relationship* with God.
+ Develop your own style of praying together that you both enjoy and are comfortable with.
+ Pray together before and after engaging in sexual intimacy.
+ Ask God to give you creative ideas for your prayer life.

+ + +

Prayer Walking

Life Is Lived in a Story

anne

After we were challenged to pray as a couple, we found that adding variety and creativity to our prayer lives helped us to *advance* in praying together. For example, decades ago we began to take regular prayer walks. When the kids were young, we would head out of the house pushing a stroller while our older kids raced ahead on their *Hot Wheels*. Combining exercise and fresh air was a great way to begin a spiritual discipline. And as the kids experienced being together outdoors, we enjoyed some adult conversation, caught up with each other—and prayed.

Our prayer walks included praying for our neighbors as we walked past their homes. If we saw an emergency vehicle or an accident, we prayed for the situation. When we walked past a hospital we prayed for those sick or injured. When we walked by a fire hydrant, we prayed for firefighters we knew. If we saw a funeral procession or passed a cemetery, we prayed for those grieving the loss of loved ones. In addition, we have prayer walked in specific areas of a city and asked the Holy Spirit to lead us. It's amazing what God brings to mind. Even as beginners we were surprised at how long we were able to joyfully and purposefully pray together as a couple.

God taught us so much during those years of prayer walking. There was an ease in the way we simply talked to Him as we walked. There was nothing religious about it—just simple conversation with the One we loved, the One we knew loved us.

> Nothing tends more to cement
> the hearts of Christians
> than praying together.
> Never do they love one another so well
> as when they witness the outpouring
> of each other's hearts in prayer.
> —Charles Finney

REAL LIFE Questions

1. Living in a fast-paced, stressful, noisy world can distract a person from developing a meaningful prayer life. Creating space to be still and embrace the sacred silence is an important part of learning how to listen to God's soft, still voice.[5] What are two changes you would be willing to make in order to focus on prayer by developing your listening skills?

_____

_____

2. Are you willing to set aside time to practice the spiritual discipline of prayer?

Yes_____ No_____

If yes, tell the Lord specific ways you would like to grow in your relationship with Him. Journal your desires in the space below.

_____

_____

3. What are some potential obstacles you see in praying together with your spouse?

_____

_____

REAL LIFE Couples Application

Praying together helps a couple to connect spiritually and emotionally to God and to each other.

Review the suggestions in this chapter for praying together with your spouse.

What (if any) are some of the potential obstacles you see or reservations you have about praying together with your spouse?

_____

_____

Set aside some time to discuss these together. Agree to extend grace to one another as you begin this new practice.

Schedule a specific day/time to pray together. Decide whether or not you want to take a prayer walk. Wives lead out first, then husbands follow.

After you are finished, review your experience. Share how it impacted your intimacy. Remember, a husband and wife can pray together, not because they have to—but because they get to.

Listening to God—I.O.T.L. (*Inquire of the Lord*)

Inviting God into your day by including Him, even in the little things, is one way to build intimacy with Him. Hebrews 12:25 says, "See to it that you do not refuse Him who is speaking." In other words, God *is* speaking, but are you taking the time to listen? At the end of each chapter, we include a *Listening to God* section. This provides an opportunity to *Inquire of the Lord* (**I.O.T.L.**) and ask the following questions:

+ *Lord, is there anything You want to highlight for me in this section?*

+ *Is there a specific step You want me to take?*

+ *Is there anything You would like me to share with my spouse?*

+ Journal anything you sense the Lord may be saying to you.

CHAPTER 16

LEAVING A PRAYER LEGACY

Life Is Lived in a Story

anne

When I fell in love with Tim in my early twenties, I knew I was marrying a man of integrity and character. But even then, we had no way of knowing what direction our lives would take. Nor could we have predicted how important our relationship with God and each other would become.

At that time, I would have described Tim as a passionate person. The type of man who is *all in* once he makes the decision to commit. Well, that approach to life was also true with his relationship with God. The Bible describes David as *a man after God's own heart*.[1] And that's how I would describe Tim.

In a marriage relationship, each spouse has a front row seat to the story God is telling through their lives. In our early years, I had an opportunity to observe Tim consistently pursuing God through his prayer life. What began as a discipline evolved into an ongoing conversation with a good Father.

Once Tim aligns with truth, he is ready to move forward. Colossians 4:2 says, "Devote yourself to prayer"—and so he did. In fact, some of my earliest memories of Tim praying were in our first home. I can still recall the large wingback chair in the corner of our living room. In the early morning hours, while everyone was still asleep, Tim would head out to the living room with his Bible in hand. As a disciplined list *pray-er*, he would get on his knees in front of that chair and pray for people by name. Often, our kids would wake up and wander into the living room half asleep. When they saw their daddy praying, they knew not to disturb him. They would turn around and run down the hallway toward our bedroom to snuggle next to me. If I asked them why they jumped in bed with me, they would say, "Daddy's praying—for me!"

Tim's ongoing conversation with God continued through the years. Regardless of where we lived or what was happening in our lives, his connection to His good Father was consistent. He not only prays for me, but also for each of our children, for their spouses, and now for our grandchildren. Praying has never been a religious duty for Tim. And it's more than just an ongoing conversation. Prayer is part of the legacy we are leaving to the next generation. James 5:16 (NIV) reminds us, "The prayer of a righteous person is powerful and effective."

The truth is, I will never fully understand (this side of heaven) what Tim's prayers on our behalf protected us from. There is no way to measure the value of the countless blessings that result from someone being willing to stand in the gap for others.[2]

The Bible makes bold statements about prayer when it says, "Devote yourselves to prayer,"[3] and, "The prayer of a righteous person is powerful and effective."[4] Throughout my growing up years, I always considered my dad as a praying man. Then, I married a man who is passionate about prayer. And as I review my life, I consider the prayers of these men as a tremendous blessing in my life.

✦ ✦ ✦

Words are powerful—and *prayer is powerful*. The Bible makes a number of bold promises. One says: "*If* My people who are called by My name will humble themselves, and *pray* and seek My face, and turn from their wicked ways, *then* I will hear from heaven, and will forgive their sin and heal their land."[5] Another passage says, "How could one man chase a thousand, or two put ten thousand to flight...?"[6]

In marriage there is a multiplication of power in the *togetherness* of *two becoming one*.[7] In our experience, husbands and wives who regularly pray together *advance* in intimacy, and together as a couple they can become a spiritual powerhouse.

But, don't take our word for it. We challenge every couple to develop a prayer strategy for their marriage. Practically, utilize some of the things we've suggested. For example, grow in your listening-to-God skills. Practice praying with your spouse, go on a prayer walk, find a prayer mentor, or develop a small prayer shield team for your marriage and family. Others of you may want to begin by writing out a detailed prayer list—and regularly praying through it.

Faithful prayers have limitless potential. *Advancing* in your prayer life will result in generational blessings being passed down to your children, grandchildren, and future generations.

But, be forewarned, when you commit to pray—expect resistance from the enemy. Recognize, renounce, and reject the enemy's schemes. Stand strong, put on the full armor of God,[8] and clothe yourself with God's mantle of humility.[9] Remember, greater is He who is in you than he who is in the world.[10]

REAL LIFE Questions

1. James 5:16b (NIV) says, "The prayer of a righteous person is powerful and effective." Give an example of a time when someone prayed for you or a time when you prayed for someone else.

_____

_____

In what specific ways were those prayers powerful and effective?

_____

_____

2. Consider the prayer legacy you are leaving to the next generation. What steps are you willing to take today in order to begin to walk that out? Be specific:

_____

_____

REAL LIFE Couples Application

In marriage, there is so much power in the togetherness of two becoming one.[11] Our experience is that husbands and wives who pray together also advance in intimacy. But, don't take our word for it. We challenge every couple to develop a prayer strategy for your marriage that includes praying together. Journal your thoughts below.

_____

_____

List two next steps you are willing to take in order for your prayer strategy to become a reality.

_____

_____

As you continue to walk out your commitment to pray, take note of how it impacts you, your life, your marriage, and your family. Journal any thoughts.

_____

_____

Listening to God—I.O.T.L. (*Inquire of the Lord*)

Inviting God into your day by including Him, even in the little things, is one way to build intimacy with Him. Hebrews 12:25 says, "See to it that you do not refuse Him who is speaking." In other words, God *is* speaking, but are you taking the time to listen? At the end of each chapter, we include a *Listening to God* section. This provides an opportunity to *Inquire of the Lord* (I.O.T.L.) and ask the following questions:

+ *Lord, is there anything You want to highlight for me in this section?*

_____

+ *Is there a specific step You want me to take?*

_____

+ *Is there anything You would like me to share with my spouse?*

_____

+ Journal anything you sense the Lord may be saying to you.

_____

_____

CHAPTER 17

25 THINGS THAT CAN HINDER PRAYERS

We believe every person can do their part to work at addressing things that can hinder their prayers. Following are 25 areas we challenge you to prayerfully explore—especially as to how they relate to your prayer life.

1. NOT ASKING can hinder your prayers. As simple as this sounds, an unasked prayer will never be answered. The Bible says, "You do not have because you do not *ask*."[1] Another passage says, "*Ask* and it will be given to you; *seek* and you will find; *knock* and the door will be opened to you. For everyone who *asks* receives; the one who *seeks* finds; and to the one who *knocks*, the door will be opened."[2]

    Regarding prayer and God, Frederick Buechner shares an interesting perspective:

    > Whatever else it may or may not be, prayer is at least talking to yourself, and that's in itself not always a bad idea. Talk to yourself about your own life, about what you've done and what you've failed to do, and about who you are and who you wish you were and who the people you love are and the people you don't love too. Talk to yourself about what matters most to you, because if you don't, you may forget what matters most to you. Even if you don't believe anybody's listening, at least you'll be listening.[3]

    The bottom line is, the first step in advancing in your prayer life is to pray.

2. WRONG MOTIVES can hinder your prayers. The Bible says, "And if you ask, you won't receive it for you're asking with corrupt motives, seeking only to fulfill your own selfish desires.[4] Having wrong motives often connects to selfishness. Part of human nature is to regard your own interests ahead of the interests of others. The Bible warns,

"Do nothing out of *selfish ambition* or vain conceit. Rather, in humility value others above yourselves, not looking to your own interests but each of you to the interests of the others."[5] Additionally, we often place our own interests ahead of God's.

3. PRIDE can hinder your prayers. The Bible gives a stern warning about pride: "God is opposed to the proud, but gives grace to the humble."[6] We don't know about you, but we don't want to do anything that results in God being opposed to us. Our real life experience is the more a person walks in a lifestyle of humility, the more they receive God's grace. And this becomes the pathway to increased intimacy and results in developing a rich and powerful prayer life.

4. UNFORGIVENESS can hinder your prayers. "And when you stand praying, if you hold anything against anyone, forgive them, so that your Father in heaven may forgive you your sins."[7] There is so much that relates to forgiveness. For example, unforgiveness is often connected to pride, control, and unrighteous judgment.[8]

5. DOUBT can hinder your prayers. The Bible says, "If any of you lacks wisdom, let him ask of God, who gives to all generously without reproach, and it will be given him. But let him ask in faith, without any doubting, for the one who doubts is like the surf of the sea, driven and tossed by the wind. For that person ought not to expect that he will receive anything from the Lord."[9] Doubt is the opposite of faith.

6. LACK OF FAITH can hinder your prayers. Prayer intimately relates to *faith*, "and whatever you ask in *prayer*, you will receive, if you have *faith*."[10] A person's prayers cannot be separated from their faith. When we ask God, we ask in faith, believing in our heart of hearts that God will listen and respond to our prayers. You can pray for anything, and if you have faith, you will receive it.[11] Of course, sometimes what we receive, or don't receive, is not what we prayed for.

The reality is a person can put their faith in just about anything. Looking back over decades of prayers, we have never regretted putting our faith in God. He has proven Himself to be powerful, good, trustworthy—and faithful.

Faith requires a measure of trust. One of our favorite Bible texts is Proverbs 3:5–8. We particularly like The Passion Translation, which says:

> Trust in the Lord completely, and do not rely on your own opinions. With all your heart rely on him to guide you, and he will lead you in every decision you make. Become intimate with him in whatever you do, and he will lead you wherever you go. Don't think for a moment that you know it all, for wisdom comes when you adore him with undivided devotion and avoid everything that's wrong. Then you will find the healing refreshment your body and spirit long for.[12]

7. NOT BELIEVING can hinder your prayers. We often remind one another that believing is a choice. That's why it is important to determine *what* you believe, as well as *who* you believe in. We resonate with John Eldredge when he writes,

> I don't think we fully understand just how much believing is a choice. Some mornings you wake and feel God is near; the day looks hopeful. Next morning God seems far; the day has no color to it. For years I wrote this experience off to the ins and outs of the spiritual life, clouded by the weather of my emotions. Then Jesus began to show me something.
>
> Innumerable times in the past several years, I'd be in a time of prayer, asking God's help or guidance with something or other, and Jesus would reply, *Believe me*. Just that—a direct command. Believe. So simple, yet it cut straight to the core of my problems. Either my wayward emotions had taken charge, or my circumstances had completely arrested my attention, but I was not settled in believing God. Nor was I operating from the position of believing God. *Believe.* The instruction revealed that I was caught up in my emotional state. Taking the simple command as the doorway back to experiencing God, I would simply say, "Okay—right. I believe you. I believe you." And Jesus would come again into my awareness. I was startled by how direct the connection was.

We wait to be struck by lightning. We wait for an epiphany. In our therapeutic age, we've become so self-conscious, so deeply entangled in our personal experiences, we think belief is also an experience, something we mostly feel. It is not. It is first and foremost an act of the will. A choice. Why else would Jesus handle the doubts of his dear friend Thomas with the command, "stop doubting and believe?" (John 20:27). Thomas had a decision to make in that moment, a decision he was quite capable of making, a decision our Lord was *waiting* for him to make. Thomas's experience was waiting on a choice.

Faith, or belief, can only be rewarded if it's something we've chosen. You don't reward your child for finishing their homework if you did it for them. Faith can't be rewarded if it simply falls on us from above. Belief is something we muster, set ourselves to, and *practice*. Especially when the "data" before us seems to argue against it. Our faith in God is our most precious possession, and God is committed to deepening and strengthening it.[13]

To sum it up, *faith* in God connects to *trusting* and *believing* in God.

8. FEAR can hinder your prayers. Often when a person lacks faith they struggle with fear. The Bible says, "There is no fear in love. But perfect love drives out fear."[14] Jesus Christ is perfect love—and He defeated fear. Likewise, in the power of the Holy Spirit—so can you.

Life Is Lived in a Story

anne + tim

We counseled a client who was doing some deep work related to fear and forgiveness. At one session he had an epiphany. The Holy Spirit showed him how much focus he had placed on *fear of failing*—but his deeper fear was *fear of success*. He held a false belief system around success. He became convinced that success would destroy him, just like it did to so many successful people in his life.

His healing journey included being able to recognize, resist, renounce, and reject this *ungodly belief* and ask the Holy Spirit to help him re-write a new *godly belief*. For example, his *godly belief* related to success was: *Success is from my good Father. It points me back to Him. I will choose to listen to the Holy Spirit and surround myself with a godly team of people who will hold me accountable with whatever measure of success God brings me.*[15]

9. NOT BEING IN COMMUNITY can hinder your prayers. We are created in the image of our good Father who exists in community. That means that we are made to thrive in relationship with others. The Bible reminds us about the importance of community.

    Proverbs 27:17 (NIV) says, "As iron sharpens iron, so one person sharpens another." Part of sharpening others and being sharpened by them includes prayer.

    Galatians 6:2 (NIV) says, "Carry each other's burdens, and in this way you will fulfill the law of Christ." Praying for those we are in community with is a way we carry their burdens.

    James 5:16 (NIV), "Therefore confess your sins to each other and pray for each other so that you may be healed. The prayer of a righteous person is powerful and effective." In this verse we can see the power that community plays in a person's prayer life.

    Acts 2:42–47 (NIV) reminds us how important community is. In verse 42 it says, "They devoted themselves to the apostles' teaching and to fellowship, to the breaking of bread and to prayer." In the Acts church, prayer was one of the main focuses in a person's life.

10. SIN can hinder your prayers. The *Oxford Dictionary* defines *sin* as "an immoral act considered to be a transgression against divine law." *Iniquity* is an "immoral or grossly unfair behavior." What does the Bible say about sin and iniquities?

But your *iniquities* have separated you from your God; and your *sins* have hidden His face from you, so that He will not hear.[16]

If I regard *iniquity* in my heart, the Lord will not hear.[17]

Because of your *sins*, he has turned away and will not listen anymore.[18]

Behold, the LORD's hand is not shortened, that it cannot save; neither his ear heavy, that it cannot hear: But your *iniquities* have separated between you and your God, and your *sins* have hid his face from you, that he will not hear.[19]

It's valuable to examine your heart to see if you have any unconfessed sins or iniquities. *Why?* Because refusing to confess your sins to God can hinder your prayers. The Psalmist writes, "If I had not confessed the sin in my heart, the Lord would not have listened."[20] In addition to examining your heart, it is also wise to ask God to reveal your sins to you. In our experience, God often reveals sin as a person reads and studies the Bible. Another suggestion is to ask those closest to you—if you are married, begin with your spouse. Ask what they have observed about the ways you live your life.

11. PAIN AND SUFFERING can hinder your prayers. When a person is experiencing difficult times, it can negatively impact their prayer life. Often the enemy uses difficult times and suffering to create distance between you and God. He tries to convince you that you are all alone. Believing the enemy's lies adds to a person's pain and suffering. And while pain and suffering may keep a person from praying, it doesn't stop God from working in a person's heart and life. Psalm 147:3 says, "God heals the brokenhearted and binds up their wounds." Even in our darkest times, God is with us, healing and binding our wounds.

Second Corinthians 1:3–4 (NIV) says we are created for community—especially during times of pain and suffering. It reads, "Praise be to the God and Father of our Lord Jesus Christ, the Father of compassion and the God of all comfort, who comforts us in all our troubles, so that we can comfort those in any trouble with the comfort we ourselves receive from God."

It is important, when dealing with pain and suffering, not to discount, deny, suppress, or repress your situation and circumstances. Remember, God has given every person the ability to feel feelings, and *when you bury a feeling—you bury it alive*. Therefore, express your feelings—but express them in healthy ways. Most importantly, invite God into your process (**I.O.T.L.**) and let Him lead you through trials and suffering. Ask God to provide a *team* of trustworthy friends and trained people to walk with you. Frederick Buechner makes a bold statement, "You have to suffer in order to be beautiful."[21]

12. BEING BLAMEWORTHY can hinder your prayers. According to the Oxford Dictionary, being *blameworthy* means being "responsible for wrongdoing and deserving of censure or blame." Do you live your life in *blameless ways*? The Bibles says, "For the LORD God is a sun and shield; the Lord bestows favor and honor; no good thing does he withhold from those whose walk is *blameless*.[22]

13. FAILING TO HONOR PARENTS can hinder your prayers. The English Standard Bible reads, "Honor your father and mother [this is the first commandment with a promise], that it may go well with you and that you may live long in the land."[23] We understand that relationships can be complicated. But honoring a parent can be walked out in many different ways. It doesn't always mean that a child will enjoy a close relationship with a parent. In our imperfect world, there may be times when a parent exhibits behavior that is toxic and unhealthy. In these instances, it is wise for a child to get help so they can establish and maintain firm boundaries. Honoring a toxic parent may include being separated from them for a time, but continuing to pray for them. Honoring parents may include going to counseling so you can work through some of the unhealed pain connected to your relationship with them.

The Bible says there are benefits for those who make an intentional choice to honor their parents. The benefits are connected to the spiritual law of *sowing and reaping*. The Bible says, "....For whatever a man *sows*, this he will also *reap*."[24] This is true of relationships. When a child sows a life of honor by relating to their parents in godly ways, they are blessed. In addition, their choice to respect, love, serve, and pray for their parents becomes a model for the next generation.

Choosing to dishonor a parent also has consequences. It can involve both active and passive choices. Active dishonor includes hurtful things a child does to their parents. Passive dishonor can be things a child fails to do for a parent. We challenge you to ask the Lord, *How does the way I treat my mom and dad impact my life?* Listen and respond as the Holy Spirit leads.

14. PERFECTIONISM can hinder your prayers, and it is often intertwined with impatience and hectic schedules. In addition, overwork, stress, and the insane pace of many peoples' lives can hinder prayers. Mother Theresa writes, "We need to find God, and he cannot be found in noise and restlessness. God is the friend of silence. See how nature—trees, flowers, grass—grows in silence; see the stars, the moon and the sun, how they move in silence... We need silence to be able to touch souls."[25]

Decades of counseling experiences suggest that people who do not have time to *pray* and *listen* to their good Father often struggle with anxiety, stress, drama, trauma, depression, and an overall dissatisfaction with life.

The famous rock band *Queen* declared, "I want it all and I want it now."[26] People can bring that demanding and perfectionist attitude to their prayer lives. *They want what they pray for—and they want it now!* But God is never in a hurry. I (tim) am a life-long *recovering idealist with perfectionist tendencies*. Two of my favorite quotes about perfectionism are, "Perfectionism rarely begets perfection, or satisfaction—only disappointment."[27] And Dr. Brené Brown writes, "Perfectionism is not the same thing as striving to be our best. Perfectionism is not about healthy achievement and growth; it's a shield."[28]

15. GIVING UP can hinder your prayers. Do you remember the story in an earlier chapter about "Royal," our friend who became the Kansas City Royals batboy? He was a quintessential model of persistence. Sadly, when we work with couples, often they develop a *throw in the towel and give up* attitude. And this becomes an obstacle to healing, advancing in intimacy, and praying persistently. Frederick Buechner writes:

> According to Jesus, by far the most important thing about praying is to keep at it. The images he uses to explain this are all rather comic, as though he thought it was rather comic to have to explain it at all. He says God is like a friend you go to borrow bread from at midnight. The friend tells you in effect to drop dead, but you go on knocking anyway until finally he gives you what you want so he can go back to bed again (Luke 11:5–8). Or God is like a crooked judge who refuses to hear the case of a certain poor widow, presumably because he knows there's nothing much in it for him. But she keeps on hounding him until finally he hears her case just to get her out of his hair (Luke 18:1–8). Even a stinker, Jesus says, won't give his own child a black eye when the child asks for peanut butter and jelly, so how all the more will God when *his* children... (Matthew 7:9–11)"[29]

We get that life can be difficult—and *stuff* happens. That said, we resonate with key points in a sermon preached by our daughter Colleen, in which she said, "Choose to keep moving forward, regardless of circumstances, because God is good—and He is good to you."[30]

16. A HUSBAND NOT HONORING HIS WIFE can hinder his prayers. The Bible says, "You husbands in the same way, live with your wives in an *understanding way*, as with someone weaker, since she is a woman; and *show her honor* as a *fellow heir* of the grace of life, *so that your prayers will not be hindered*."[31] Husbands review that passage and maybe re-read chapter 14 of this book, "Husbands Are Your Prayers Hindered?" to see if your behaviors—including not living with your bride in an *understanding way* and *honoring her as a fellow heir and co-leader*—might be *hindering your prayers*.

17. DISUNITY can hinder your prayers. After over forty-three years of marriage, we have experienced the benefits of *walking in unity*. When we are tracking together with God and each other, we describe the benefits in our marriage as feeling like God enables us to become a spiritual powerhouse. And this impacts every area in our lives—including our prayer life.

There is power in relationships and unity: "How could one single enemy chase a thousand of them, and two put ten thousand to flight, unless their Rock had abandoned them, unless the Lord had destroyed them?"[32] Throughout decades of counseling, we have observed that disunity weakens a couple's intimacy and oneness, and this negatively impacts their prayer life.

18. LACK OF SELF-CARE can hinder your prayers. Often, when we talk about prayer with husbands, wives, and couples, they sigh and say, "Frankly, my life is so full, I just don't have enough time or energy to pray!" The truth is, every person has 24 hours in their day. And each day is made up of choices that a person makes. However, making good choices requires personal health.

Prayer can be a form of self-care. It's the evidence that you are relying on God. Prayer grounds a person, connects them with their good Father, and invites them to live in the Larger Story (where God is the main character) rather than living in the smaller story (where they are the main character). We resonate with what Parker Palmer writes, "Self-care is never a selfish act—it is simply good stewardship of the only gift I have, the gift I was put on earth to offer others. Anytime we can listen to true self and give the care it requires, we do it not only for ourselves, but for the many others whose lives we touch."[33]

It's valuable to distinguish between self-care and self-soothing behaviors and activities. Paul Byerly writes:

> Self-soothing is doing things that make us feel better. It could be eating, exercise, sex, drinking or drugs, playing video games, or many other things.

Some of what we do to self-sooth is sinful and/or harmful, while some is not. Self-soothing is not inherently wrong, but it does nothing to remove a problem or help us find a way to resolve problems. Even if our self-soothing doesn't hurt us, if we just do it to escape it is or will become a problem.

Self-care is about realizing our valid needs and making those a priority. It means finding safe and sane ways to meet those needs without hurting us or those around us. Some of what is done as self-soothing can also be self-care, but the motive and approach is different.

Self-care is also about growth. It may give us needed stress relief and it may clear our minds so we can focus better. But it's not about denying or hiding from reality.[34]

Another thing that can connect to self-care and inhibit your prayers is *not being kind to yourself*. We work with clients who are harder on themselves than anyone else in their lives. When chaos surfaces, they quickly default to shaming themselves, which leads to blame, fear, and control. With a desire to push-back against shame—which the enemy would love to become a person's false identity—and being overly self-critical, we give them a print-out and encourage them to read it every day. It reads:

BE KIND TO MYSELF
BE KIND TO MYSELF
BE KIND TO MYSELF
BE KIND TO MYSELF
BE KIND TO MYSELF

Allowing truth to wash over you is an important initial step in healing. It also silences the lies of the enemy.

19. NOT GUARDING YOUR HEART AND TONGUE can hinder your prayers. When the Bible says, "*Above all else guard your heart,*"[35] that gets our attention. Guarding

your *heart* includes inviting God into your process (**I.O.T.L.**), keeping your priorities straight, establishing and maintaining healthy boundaries, and letting the love of God guide you.

Guarding your tongue is every bit as important. Think about the words that come out of your mouth. *Are they often toxic, critical, and life-draining—or loving, encouraging, and life-giving?* The Bible talks about the power in a person's tongue. James 3:5-10 (NIV) says:

> The tongue is a small part of the body, but it makes great boasts. Consider what a great forest is set on fire by a small spark. The tongue also is a fire, a world of evil among the parts of the body. It corrupts the whole body, sets the whole course of one's life on fire, and is itself set on fire by hell. All kinds of animals, birds, reptiles and sea creatures are being tamed and have been tamed by mankind, but no human being can tame the tongue. It is a restless evil, full of deadly poison. With the tongue we praise our Lord and Father, and with it we curse human beings, who have been made in God's likeness. Out of the same mouth come praise and cursing. My brothers and sisters, this should not be.

Are you up for a challenge? Study the verse, "The mouth speaks out of that which fills the heart,"[36] and monitor the words you speak for thirty days. **I.O.T.L.** and ask the Holy Spirit to help you evaluate the words you speak. If they are positive, encouraging, and life-giving, thank God and continue to use your words to bless others. And if your words are unkind, mean, or toxic, talk with a mature friend, mentor, or counselor to help you process any negativity in your heart.

20. NOT BEING THANKFUL can impact your prayers. The Bible says:

> Rejoice in the Lord always. I will say it again: Rejoice! Let your gentleness be evident to all. The Lord is near. Do not be anxious about anything, but in every situation, by prayer and petition, with *thanksgiving*, present your requests to

God. And the peace of God, which transcends all understanding, will guard your hearts and your minds in Christ Jesus. Finally, brothers and sisters, whatever is true, whatever is noble, whatever is right, whatever is pure, whatever is lovely, whatever is admirable—if anything is excellent or praiseworthy—think about such things.[37]

In our experience, couples, families, friends, and clients who have thankful hearts—and who presuppose the best in others—have rich prayer lives.

21. THE ENEMY can inhibit your prayers. The Bible warns, "Our struggle is not against flesh and blood, but against the rulers, against the authorities, against the powers of this dark world and against the spiritual forces of evil in the heavenly realms."[38] It continues, "And pray in the Spirit on all occasions with all kinds of prayers and requests. With this in mind, be alert and always keep on praying for all the Lord's people. Pray also for me, that whenever I speak, words may be given me so that I will fearlessly make known the mystery of the gospel, for which I am an ambassador in chains. Pray that I may declare it fearlessly, as I should."[39] It's obvious that the apostle Paul understood the reality of spiritual warfare and the importance of always praying in the Spirit—and so should we.

22. NOT UNDERSTANDING YOUR TRUE IDENTITY can hinder your prayers. We cannot overemphasize the importance of understanding and living out *your true identity*. You are God's *beloved* son or daughter. Put this book down for a moment, take a deep breath, and declare out loud, "*I* [your name] *am God's beloved son/daughter*." Children who know they are loved by God have more intimate relationships, and in that security their prayer life increases in intimacy and power. Oswald Chambers wrote:

> Prayer is one of God's vital means of transforming us into Christlikeness in every aspect of our lives (2 Cor. 3:18). Beloved, the ultimate purpose of prayer is not to simple change your situations, but primarily to increasingly change you into who God intended you to be (Christ-like).[40]

In our experience, the more a person understands their true identity, the more they understand that they are God's favorite. And this leads to a lifestyle of humility, which we believe is a key ingredient to a healthy and kingdom-advancing prayer life.

Life Is Lived in a Story

tim

I was recently at a counseling session—yes, I go to counseling. <smile> In fact, Anne and I often say, *"Don't see a counselor who doesn't see a counselor!"* A recent session began with my counselor asking, "Tim, as I'm counseling clients, I'm doing some research. And I ask each of them the same question, *What is a foundational truth in your life right now?* How about you—*what is a foundational truth in your life right now?*"

I paused, did a quick **I.O.T.L.**, and replied, "I would have to say that after walking with Jesus for decades, I truly believe that *I am God's favorite!*"

My counselor appeared stunned, she shook her head back-and-forth and replied, "Wow—it's so refreshing for me to hear you say that. I can't begin to imagine how living life believing *I am God's favorite* would be a game-changer for me. Not to mention how it would influence my husband, kids, friends—and clients."

The reality is if a person understands their true identity—that they are God's *beloved* son or daughter—this can help them to realize they are God's favorite. Okay, we understand the concept of being God's favorite may be difficult for some readers to comprehend. Remember, God's unfathomable and unconditional love is related to the mystery in His character. That said, as we walk out being God's favorites, we pray that each of our children and grandchildren will experience what it's like to live their lives believing—in their heart of hearts—that *they are God's favorite!*

How about you? How would you answer the question, *What is a foundational truth in your life right now?* We suspect your answer is related, in one way or another, to your understanding of your true identity.

23. NOT UNDERSTANDING GOD'S IDENTITY can hinder your prayers. We encourage clients to focus on *God's identity* rather than on how you perceive His *behavior*. We believe to the fabric of our souls that *God is good and He can be trusted*. And the longer we walk with the Lord, the more we trust life's unknowns and unanswered questions to our trustworthy God.[41]

24. YOU can hinder your prayers. Can *you* be the answer to any of the prayer requests you are praying? For example, say a friend asks you to pray about something they need. If you have the ability and/or resources to meet that need, and you sense God inviting you to meet it, rather than agreeing to pray—what if *you* simply met the need?

Another example: We have worked with people who regularly prayed for financial blessings. Certainly, praying for financial blessings can be important. But, in addition to praying, we challenge them to review the areas of their life they can control while they are praying for the things they can't control. For example, review what the Bible says about giving joyfully, tithing, sacrificial giving, first-fruits, and other principles of godly stewardship. We encourage them to make observations about how they steward the money they already have. Then take ownership and responsibility for any changes they may need to make.

Instead of inordinately focusing on God providing additional finances, determine strategic ways to either reduce spending or acquire more income. Of course, this type of thinking must include a measure of humility. But our experience is the more a person walks in a lifestyle of humility, the more rich and powerful their prayer life becomes.

25. LACK OF LOVE can hinder your prayers. The older we get, the more we believe that *love is the ballgame*. Jesus was asked, "Which is the greatest commandment in the Law?" He replied, "'Love the Lord your God with all your heart and with all your soul and with all your mind.' This is the first and greatest commandment. And the second is like it: 'Love your neighbor as yourself.' All the Law and the Prophets hang

on these two commandments."[42] Additional love passages say, "Love never fails,"[43] and, "The greatest of these is love."[44]

In our experience, the most loving people we know understand the command to "devote yourselves to prayer, being watchful and thankful."[45] And as a person focuses on prayer, as they are watchful and thankful, they advance in intimacy with God. And this results in becoming more loving as they advance in intimacy with others—and advance in their prayer life.

Practically, this involves purposefully living out the command to *abide in Christ*. In the Bible, Jesus commands His followers, "Abide in me, and I in you."[46] *Abide* is an active verb. Therefore, abiding in Christ involves ongoing moment-by-moment decisions that a person makes to *not* let feelings or circumstances direct their lives. Practically, this includes trusting *everything* to your good Father, God.

Later in John 15, *abiding in Christ* is compared to a vine and a branch. The branch represents people, and in order to survive they must be intimately connected to God—the Vine. When a person is connected to Christ, they can receive nurture, sustenance, and the ability to reproduce—to bear much fruit.

REAL LIFE Questions

1. UNFORGIVENESS can hinder your prayers. Unforgiveness is often connected to pride, control, and unrighteous judgment. When you think of someone who is difficult to pray for, is any unforgiveness in place? If so, what is one next step you can take to deal with unforgiveness?

_____

_____

_____

2. SIN can hinder your prayers. The Bible says, "But your *iniquities* have separated you from your God; and your *sins* have hidden His face from you, so that He will not hear."[47] Another translation says, "But your iniquities have made a separation between you and your God, and your sins have hidden His face from you so that He does not hear"[48]

Is there any ongoing sin in your life? If yes, what is one strategic step you can take to deal with this sin?

_____

_____

Do you feel like God doesn't listen to you? If yes, could this be connected to unconfessed sin?

_____

_____

3. LACK OF SELF-CARE can hinder your prayers. Have you ever viewed your prayer life as a form of self-care? Yes _____ No_____ What is one way you can advance in taking care of your soul?

_____

_____

_____

4. GIVING UP can hinder your prayers. Take some time to **I.O.T.L.** and ask the Holy Spirit to show you any prayers you have given up on. Write them down, and consider praying these prayers once again. Journal your thoughts.

_____

_____

5. FAILING TO HONOR PARENTS can hinder your prayers. What comes to your heart and mind when you hear the command *honor your parents*?

_____

_____

Overall, are things *going well with you?* Consider how the way you treat your dad and mom (and father-in-law and mother-in-law) connects to your life going well—or not going well. Journal your thoughts

_____

_____

_____

What is one way you can purposefully *honor your parents?*

_____

_____

6. Review the other things in this chapter that can hinder prayer.

Which areas are you doing well in?

_____

_____

_____

Which areas do you struggle with? Briefly explain your struggles.

_____

_____

What is one strategic step you can take to deal with each of the ones you listed above.

_____

_____

REAL LIFE Couples Application

DISUNITY can hinder your prayers. The authors say they "are 100 percent convinced of the amazing benefits of co-leading together and walking *in unity*." Think of a time when you and your spouse walked together in unity. What was the outcome?

_____

_____

Each of you list one way you can advance in living together in unity?

_____

_____

Listening to God—I.O.T.L. (*Inquire of the Lord*)

Inviting God into your day by including Him, even in the little things, is one way to build intimacy with Him. Hebrews 12:25 says, "See to it that you do not refuse Him who is speaking." In other words, God *is* speaking, but are you taking the time to listen? At the end of each chapter, we include a *Listening to God* section. This provides an opportunity to *Inquire of the Lord* (**I.O.T.L.**) and ask the following questions:

+ *Lord, is there anything You want to highlight for me in this section?*

_____

+ *Is there a specific step You want me to take?*

_____

+ *Is there anything You would like me to share with my spouse?*

_____

+ Journal anything you sense the Lord may be saying to you.

_____

_____

CHAPTER 18

WHAT IF MY PRAYERS ARE NOT ANSWERED IN THE WAY I WANT?

Throughout this book we have addressed many different aspects of prayer. However, a book on prayer would not be complete without addressing an important question that everyone asks at some point: *What if my prayers are not answered in the ways I want?*

Have you ever made a prayer request that was *not* answered in the way you desired? The truth is God has not answered many of the prayers we've prayed. For example, we have prayed for people to be healed from sickness and disease—but some of them remained sick and died. We know couples who prayed to become pregnant and have a biological child—but they are still childless. We've worked with couples who were struggling in their marriage, and they passionately prayed for their marriage to be restored—but they ended up getting divorced.

Often prayers we consider *unanswered* tend to raise more questions than provide answers. To clarify, when we label a prayer *unanswered*, what we mean is our prayer was not answered in the way *we* hoped for—and in the way *we* wanted it to be answered.

Life Is Lived in a Story

anne

Early in our marriage, Tim served in the middle school student ministry with a young woman in her twenties. Over time we all became close friends. She spent a lot of time with our family. Then, she received a terminal cancer diagnosis and was facing the decision to be admitted into hospice. She asked Tim and me if she could move into our home. She wanted to spend her last days surrounded by friends who had become family to her. At that time, we had four children under the age of twelve. We wondered what impact this decision would have on our family and how it would affect our daily life. Tim and I prayed, sought counsel, and decided in unity to have her move into our home.

Looking back, that five-month journey taught us how to pray in new ways. We set up her hospital bed in the family room. It was accessible to visitors who regularly stopped by to encourage her. As she fought for her life, people gathered in our home to pray. Teams of intercessors would sit around her bed declaring healing Scriptures over her. I will always remember the evening a group of women from a local church stopped by to visit. They sang songs of praise and worship over her and boldly asked on her behalf for God to heal her. In those days, our home became a sanctuary as the prayers of the righteous infused peace, hope, and faith into all of our hearts.

God used our prayers and our conversations to teach us about His goodness. What I learned in that season, I still carry with me today. It took a terminal diagnosis for me to discover a depth of God's goodness that I had never known before. But in spite of our best efforts, early one morning before the sun rose, she died in our home. While our prayers for healing and complete restoration were not answered this side of heaven—we believe they were answered.

Her death stirred up so many questions. We believed with all of our hearts that what the Bible said was true. We were holding on with faith that, "If you *believe*, you will *receive* whatever you *ask* for in prayer."[1] We did just that; we *prayed*, we *believed*, and we—along with many others—*asked* God to heal our friend.

But we did not *receive* what we asked for. Many times, we wondered *why*. We knew God could heal; we just didn't know *why* He didn't heal. Or, looking back, did He? Was her healing answered the moment she slipped out of our arms and into His? While we didn't have any answers, we knew that even if we did, they would fall short in light of her death. In the days that followed, we chose to trust God. And we made the volitional choice to believe He is good.

People are continually praying, asking in faith, and believing. The truth is, a person may never receive the answers they are hoping for. The enemy is quick to fill in the gap with questions and introduce doubt. Prayers not answered in the way a person desires can lead them to question, *If God is all powerful—which I believe He is—then why doesn't He stop bad things from happening? And if God is good—which I believe He is—then how can He let so many horrible things happen?*

+ + +

Where to Begin Addressing Questions

A person can begin anything in one of three ways:

1. They can begin with what *others* think.
2. They can begin with what *they* think.
3. They can begin with what the *Bible* says about a topic.

Let's briefly look at what others say about prayer.

Oswald Chambers (author of *My Utmost for His Highest*) wrote, "Our Lord never referred to unanswered prayer; he taught that prayers are always answered."[2]

Best-selling author Anne Lamont wrote, "I've seen prayers answered. But often, in my experiences, if you get what you pray for, you've really shortchanged yourself."[3]

Author Jim George wrote, "When your prayers aren't answered immediately, sometimes God has a different—or better—plan."[4]

Lloyd John Ogilvie wrote, "All our prayers are answered, we need to distinguish between a prayer unanswered, and one not answered how or when we would like it to be."[5]

Mother Teresa wrote, "Prayer is not asking. Prayer is putting oneself in the hands of God, at His disposition, and listening to His voice in the depth of our hearts."[6]

And C.S. Lewis wrote, "Prayers are not always—in the crude, factual sense of the word—'granted.' This is not because prayer is a weaker kind of causality [or power], but because it is a stronger kind. When it 'works' at all it works unlimited by space and time."[7]

We have shared what other people have written about prayer, but what does the *Bible* say about God hearing and answering our prayers?

This is the confidence we have in approaching God: that if we ask anything according to his will, He hears us.[8]

I tell you, whatever you ask for in prayer, believe that you have received it, and it will be yours.[9]

Ask and it will be given to you; seek and you will find; knock and the door will be opened to you.[10]

If you believe, you will receive whatever you ask for in prayer.[11]

For my thoughts are not your thoughts, neither are your ways my ways declares the Lord. As the heavens are higher than the earth, so are my ways higher than your ways and my thoughts than your thoughts.[12]

When we struggle with unanswered prayer, we think about the apostle Paul. He was the person who, under the inspiration of the Holy Spirit, wrote the majority of the New Testament—and he had struggles. The Bible uses the metaphor *thorn in the flesh* to describe something in Paul's life that was a continual source of pain. Paul wrote, "Three times I pleaded with the Lord to take it away from me. But he said to me, 'My grace is sufficient for you, for my power is made perfect in weakness.'" Paul went on to say, "Therefore I will boast all the more gladly about my weaknesses, so that Christ's power may rest on me."[13]

If Paul struggled with unanswered prayer, why should we be any different? We believe his challenge was, rather than focusing on his *thorn in the flesh*, he reframed his situation by placing God as the main character in his story—and not himself. His response reflected his trust in the One who is totally trustworthy.

$$+ + +$$

Creation - Fall - Redemption

Throughout our ministry, counseling, and writing, we try to frame things through a CRE-ATION – FALL – REDEMPTION narrative. Let's look at unanswered prayer through the same filter.[14]

CREATION—in creation, *in the beginning*, before sin entered the story, the man and women were both made in God's image—male and female He made them.[15] And the first thing God did after creating humans was bless them. Next, He gave the man and woman two mandates. First, the procreation mandate, "Be fruitful and increase in number." Second, the dominion (rulership) mandate, "Rule over the fish in the sea and the birds in the sky and over every living creature that moves on the ground."[16]

In the beginning, the man and woman were *both* commissioned to carry out the procreation and dominion (rulership) mandates.[17] *Together* they walked with God in the cool of the day,[18] they related with Him, and they enjoyed marital oneness (spirit+soul+body) and the sacredness of being *naked without shame*.[19] The Bible describes things in Eden—before sin entered the story—as being *very* good.[20]

FALL—However, the man and woman were not alone in the garden. There was a serpent who lied to them and questioned God's goodness.[21] The woman and man rebelled against God, and the enemy stole the dominion God had given to them. One of the first negative consequences was in marriage. Mutuality and co-leadership were replaced with the woman desiring her husband—who would *rule over her*.[22] One of the tragic results of the Fall was that the man and woman's intimacy with God and each other was fractured and fragmented.

REDEMPTION—Redemption is defined by the Oxford Dictionary as, "The action of saving or being saved from sin, error, or evil." Redemption is available through Jesus Christ:

> But when the fullness of the time came, God sent forth His Son, born of a woman, born under the Law, so that He might redeem those who were under the Law, that we might receive the adoption as sons. Because you are sons, God has sent forth the Spirit of His Son into our hearts, crying, "Abba! Father!" Therefore, you are no longer a slave, but a son; and if a son, then an heir through God.[23]

Every person has a choice to view themselves as a *slave* or as a *beloved* son or daughter. By *slave* we mean being inordinately controlled by a spouse, church, doctrine, guilt, shame, fear, anxiety, addiction, sinful behaviors, personal feelings, or your past or present.

Thankfully, in the fullness of time, God in Jesus Christ took on human form and came to earth. In power encounters with Satan, and through His death on a cross, He took back the dominion that was originally designed for the man and woman. The good news is, women and men can embrace their true identities and experience being *beloved* sons and daughters of a good God. And *together* they can reclaim the dominion (rulership) and procreation mandates.

In addition, Jesus said that it was better for Him to leave, so He could send the Holy Spirit.[24] When invited, God the Holy Spirit will indwell a person. He strengthens, encourages, comforts, guides, protects, and helps a person advance in intimacy with God. As this occurs, a person will grow in loving others. Unfortunately, even with all these good things, until Jesus Christ returns there are still lingering consequences of the Fall. And we believe this relates to the topic of this chapter: *What if my prayers are not answered in the way I want?*

+ + +

We do not have infallible—*incapable of being wrong*—answers to life's questions or to the mystery of what we perceive as unanswered prayers. Certainly, a person can do their part to eliminate things that can hinder their prayers, including the 25 things we wrote about in the previous chapter. For us personally, when we are wrestling with God to answer our prayers in the ways we want, it's easy to forget that He already knows what we truly need—and more importantly, *He is the answer*. Of course, we are never certain exactly how that will play out—but we believe 100 percent that *God is our answer*. And we can choose to surrender our desires and outcomes to Him.

Throughout our lives we have walked alongside many people who have experienced unimaginable things, including health issues, betrayal, violence, divorce, abuse, addictions, financial calamities, family suicide, and what counselors suggest is the most difficult trauma to walk through—the death of a child. And we've observed that the people who most successfully walked through their crises had two important things in common—*a faith in God that was real and family and friends who were true*. They were grounded in their faith and surrounded by a supportive community.

But...Why?

As we continue to mature in our lives (and marriage), and as we advance in intimacy with God, by His grace we find ourselves spending less time and energy trying to figure out the answers to questions that only God can answer. We have experienced enough of life to know that there are some things that we will never be able to explain this side of heaven. These things we choose to simply surrender to God—as we trust in His goodness.

The Bible goes a step further by inviting us to, "Consider it pure joy, my brothers and sisters, whenever you face trials of many kinds, because you know that the testing of your faith produces perseverance."[25] And so, we take into account that we have a choice in how we can respond. We believe God is working through each situation on our behalf, even when we have no answers. On a practical side, we also realize there are things we need to take ownership and responsibility for when it comes to the consequences we face.

We try to do our best to begin everything by inviting God into our process (**I.O.T.L.**). We focus on our faith in God—and our core belief that He is good. We also invite trustworthy family and friends into our process. For us, it has always been our faith in God and the presence of a supportive community that has gotten us through the darkest of times.

We realize that our understanding is limited. We see only in part and don't have full understanding of the story that is being told through our lives and life circumstances. Isaiah 55:8–9 says, "'For my thoughts are not your thoughts, neither are your ways my ways,' declares the Lord. 'As the heavens are higher than the earth, so are my ways higher than your ways and my thoughts than your thoughts.'"[26] We look to the truth found in God's Word for encouragement and strength by reminding ourselves we are not alone, "I am with you always, even to the end of the age."[27] God promises us, "Never will I leave you; never will I forsake you."[28]

The following *Footprints in the Sand* poem captures our hearts when we feel alone, when we are struggling with questions, or when our prayers seem unanswered.

One night a man had a dream. He dreamed
he was walking along the beach with the LORD.
Across the sky flashed scenes from his life.
For each scene he noticed two sets of
footprints in the sand: one belonging
to him, and the other to the LORD.

When the last scene of his life flashed before him,
he looked back at the footprints in the sand.
He noticed that many times along the path of
his life there was only one set of footprints.
He also noticed that it happened at the very
lowest and saddest times in his life.

This really bothered him and he
questioned the LORD about it:
"LORD, you said that once I decided to follow

you, you'd walk with me all the way.

But I have noticed that during the most

troublesome times in my life,

there is only one set of footprints.

I don't understand why when

I needed you most you would leave me."

The LORD replied:

"My son, my precious child,

I love you and I would never leave you.

During your times of trial and suffering,

when you see only one set of footprints,

it was then that I carried you."[29]

✝ ✝ ✝

There are simply no easy explanations for prayers that are not answered in the way we desire. For us, heartache and tragedies in our lives have resulted in a growing list of questions we look forward to asking the Lord about one day. Thankfully, this passage gives us hope, "For now we see only a reflection as in a mirror; then we shall see face to face. Now I know in part; then I shall know fully, even as I am fully known.[30]

There is much we don't know, but we do know one thing for certain: *God is God—and He can be trusted.* Regarding unanswered prayers we've prayed, we whole-heartedly agree with Garth Brooks' song lyric, "Some of God's greatest gifts are unanswered prayers."[31]

REAL LIFE Questions

1. Have you ever had an unanswered prayer? (Note: When we use the phrase *unanswered prayer*, we are referring to a prayer that was not answered in the way you had hoped.) If yes, what was your prayer?

_____

_____

What was the story you told yourself when your prayer was not answered in the way you desired?

_____

_____

Do you still have the same perspective? Yes_____ No_____ If No, briefly explain what changed?

_____

_____

2. A person can begin anything in one of three ways. 1. They can begin with what *others* think. 2. They can begin with what *they* think. 3. They can begin with what the *Bible says* about a topic. Make some observations about the way you typically respond to life. Which of these three ways do you most often begin with?

_____

_____

3. The Bible says, "The secret things belong to the Lord our God."[32] Make some observations: What are some of the "secret things" in your life that only God knows?

_____

_____

As you remind yourself of the *secret things* that belong to the Lord, take a moment to surrender them (once again) to Him. Journal your thoughts.

_____

_____

4. The authors write that two things have gotten them through difficult and painful times, #1 a faith in God that's real, and #2 family and friends that are true. As you review your life, what has gotten you through difficult and painful times?

_____

_____

5. Re-read the *Footprints in the Sand* poem. When were specific times the Lord carried you?

_____

_____

REAL LIFE Couples Application

Garth Brooks wrote, "Some of God's greatest gifts are unanswered prayers." Schedule a date with your spouse and together list some unanswered prayers that ended up being a blessing to you and your marriage.

How would your life be different today if those prayers were answered in the ways you desired?

_____

_____

Listening to God—I.O.T.L. (*Inquire of the Lord*)

Inviting God into your day by including Him, even in the little things, is one way to build intimacy with Him. Hebrews 12:25 says, "See to it that you do not refuse Him who is speaking." In other words, God *is* speaking, but are you taking the time to listen? At the end of each chapter, we include a *Listening to God* section. This provides an opportunity to *Inquire of the Lord* (**I.O.T.L.**) and ask the following questions:

+ *Lord, is there anything You want to highlight for me in this section?*

_____

+ *Is there a specific step You want me to take?*

_____

+ *Is there anything You would like me to share with my spouse?*

_____

+ Journal anything you sense the Lord may be saying to you.

_____

_____

CHAPTER 19

NEXT STEPS

As we look over our lives, we see ways God continues to invite us to join Him. But saying *yes* to *next steps* has required trusting Him. Our *first next step* was getting married. In the year that followed, we made the choice to explore a more personal relationship with God. That decision was followed by raising a family, investing in our careers, serving in local churches, being part of community groups, and leading in Bible studies. Personal *next steps* have included making an investment in counseling and inner healing. *Next steps* have included changing careers and living in four states (Illinois, Michigan, California, Colorado).

Over 15 years ago, we took a *next step* of co-leading REAL LIFE ministries full-time. Ongoing *day-to-day steps* include working on our own marriage while walking out our *missionaries to marriage* calling. This includes pastoral counseling, being marriage mentors, developing marriage tools, writing, leading REAL LIFE gatherings and workshops, being involved in our local church—and focusing on being fully devoted parents and grandparents.

After inviting God into our process (**I.O.T.L.**)[1] and implementing the **Traffic Light Principle**[2] *together* in unity, we have taken one *next step* after another. And with each step, our desire has been to better understand our true identities and grow in whole-heartedly loving God, others, and ourselves.[3] Concerning marriage, even after forty-three years, we are both committed to passionately living out God's creational marriage design.

+ + +

If you are a local church or ministry leader, an important *first next step* would be to strategically evaluate your current marriage culture. Generally speaking, how is marriage emphasized and lived out? How often do you teach about marriage, intimacy, and sexual discipleship? Are you proactive rather than reactive when it comes to building godly, healthy marriages?

Important questions to ask are: How much of your budget is invested in marriage enrichment, training, equipping, and mentoring? Do you lead and host regular marriage gatherings? Does your church or community of faith have paid fulltime marriage pastors?

If you are part of a church or ministry leadership team that is serious about developing a strong marriage culture, it would be worthwhile to establish some bench marks—*strategic next steps*—to take. And when determining *next steps*, it would be wise for leaders to ask, *what steps can we can take to create a healthy marriage culture in our church or community of faith?*

How about you? Are you up for a few *next step* challenges? *Paying it forward* to others is often a person's response when they have received God's unconditional love and forgiveness. As *missionaries to marriage*, we cannot overstate the importance of married couples taking strategic *next steps* to help them advance in intimacy and spirit + soul + body oneness. Practically, if investing in this *PRAYER* book has been beneficial, consider leading a marriage focused community group. Of course, there are many marriage tools available. Our encouragement is to **I.O.T.L.** and be open to going through some of the books we have invested decades working on. REAL LIFE books include:

+ **TOGETHER:** *Reclaiming Co-Leadership in Marriage* [+*Companion Journal*]

+ **NAKED:** *Reclaiming Sexual Intimacy in Marriage* [+*Companion Journal*]

+ **SOULGASM:** *Caring for Your Soul and the Soul of Your Marriage* [+*Companion Journal*]

+ **COMMUNICATION:** *A Key to Advancing in Intimacy*

+ **PRAYER:** *Talking With God*

Upcoming Books:

+ **FORGIVENESS:** *Begins With a Decision*

+ **ABUSE:** *Experiencing Freedom through Forgiveness*

If you are married, taking *next-step* challenges can become the pathway to *advancing* in intimacy with God, your spouse, and others. And for churches that purposefully invest in training and equipping their members in marriage, it will pay rich dividends. We frequently say that marriage has so much untapped kingdom-advancing potential.

+ + +

Marriage (R.I.T.) Rapid Intervention Teams
Life Is Lived in a Story

tim

I recall my counselor saying to me decades ago, "Tim, it seems that you can tend to default to being an *idealist with perfectionist tendencies*." I wasn't sure if that was good or bad—but over the years it has proven to be both.

As I continue to co-lead REAL LIFE ministries with Anne, God has used my *idealistic* bent to fuel the vision He has given us for what marriage could look like. As an *idealist with perfectionist tendencies*, I wake up and go to bed thinking about the kingdom-advancing impact that a godly marriage can have on the church, our culture—and the world. Following is one aspect of my vision for marriage.

+ + +

Throughout twenty plus years in the fire service I was blessed with a number of promotions, including Lieutenant, Captain, Battalion Chief, and I retired as a Deputy Fire Chief. As an Incident Commander, I knew that an officer and a team of firefighters would be assigned as a Rapid Intervention Team (RIT) for every major fire and emergency.

The RIT was not responsible for any of the immediate tasks required in handling the emergency. They were assigned to the incident commander and were required to remain at the command post. The team members were in full turnout gear and had all their firefighting tools and equipment. They were available at a moment's notice should anything occur that placed firefighters in danger.

If the RIT was called upon, it meant something bad had happened to their brothers and sisters fighting the fire. In any sudden emergency, such as a flashover, backdraft, or collapse, the incident commander would immediately direct the RIT to mitigate the situation.

As Anne and I consider all the support and safety fire department RITs provide, we wonder, *What would it be like if local churches developed teams specifically for couples who were struggling in their marriages?* They could be called *Marriage Rapid Intervention Teams (MRIT)*. We envision untapped kingdom-of-God impact in teams of women and men who have hearts for God, are a trained in marriage, and who understand the power in prayer.

When a couple experiences trouble,[4] the MRIT could serve as *marriage first responders*—people who are ready and available to surround and support couples who are dealing with issues that are threatening their marriage.

MRIT leaders would receive training that would be a form of discipleship. It would include a deeper understanding of your true identity, covenant, mutuality, co-leadership, the **Traffic Light Principle**, biblical grounds for divorce, and many core life-giving marriage principles. It would also cover areas such as forgiveness, communication, prayer, abuse, and God's goodness.

An essential part of training would be to equip MRIT leaders to be able to *triage* couples—*assign degrees of urgency and decide the order of emotional and spiritual support.* This would involve being able to assess a couple's immediate needs and discern whether more specialized support is needed. The MRIT could refer couples to professional counselors who specialize in issues related to adultery, addiction, abuse, trauma, PTSD, and other emergencies.

While those are more extreme examples, a MRIT could also help couples who are not dealing with major marriage trauma. They could come alongside hurting couples and share godly wisdom, provide genuine encouragement, and pray targeted prayers. All that is to say, developing a MRIT could be a strategic *next step* for churches and couples to take.

REAL LIFE Questions

1. Review your married years, list some of the key next steps God has invited you to take.

_____

_____

2. If you have a heart for marriage, what strategic next steps can you take to continue developing a healthy marriage?

_____

_____

3. If you are in church or ministry leadership and desire to develop a strong marriage culture, what strategic next steps can you take?

_____

_____

4. In this chapter, Tim described himself as an _idealist with perfectionist tendencies_. Make some observations about the vision for churches developing Marriage Rapid Intervention Teams (MRITs)?

_____

_____

Do you know of anyone who could have benefited from the support of a MRIT? If yes, what were the circumstances?

_____

_____

REAL LIFE Couples Application

What specific *next steps* are you willing to take as a couple to advance in intimacy with each other?

_____

_____

Are you willing to co-lead a marriage community group? Yes _____ No _____ If yes, what topic would you choose, and who would you invite to be a part of your marriage community?

_____

_____

Listening to God—I.O.T.L. (*Inquire of the Lord*).

Inviting God into your day by including Him, even in the little things, is one way to build intimacy with Him. Hebrews 12:25 says, "See to it that you do not refuse Him who is speaking." In other words, God *is* speaking, but are you taking the time to listen? At the end of each chapter, we include a *Listening to God* section. This provides an opportunity to *Inquire of the Lord* (**I.O.T.L.**) and ask the following questions:

+ *Lord, is there anything You want to highlight for me in this section?*

_____

+ *Is there a specific step You want me to take?*

_____

+ *Is there anything You would like me to share with my spouse?*

_____

+ Journal anything you sense the Lord may be saying to you.

_____

_____

EPILOGUE

MARRIAGE IS NOT "IT"

In every book in our REAL LIFE Marriage series, we emphasize that every marriage will experience troubles.[1] And we challenge husbands, wives, and couples to not view troubles as *obstacles*—but instead to view them as *opportunities*.

We also say in all of our books that, as much as we love marriage, as much as we have tried to live out God's *two become one*[2] and *naked without shame*[3] creational marriage design,[4] our primary *missionaries to marriage* message is not about *marriage*—but about *God*, the Maker of marriage (including God the Father + Jesus Christ + Holy Spirit).

Because Jesus Christ reclaimed the dominion (rulership) the enemy stole in the garden, we believe couples can return to God's mutuality and functional equality—*co-leadership*—principles of Paradise. And as God's creational marriage design is reclaimed and restored, it will provide opportunities—when a person asks—to share with gentleness and respect the amazing story about Jesus Christ.

The Quintessential Story

Throughout our writings, we share a number of stories. However, we believe the greatest story in all of history is the story of God visiting humans. Over 2,000 years ago God—Jesus Christ—visited humankind, and things were never the same.

Growing up, we both faithfully attended church, participated in the sacraments, and celebrated religious holidays. We were familiar with some of Jesus' story. However, as young married adults in our early twenties, we began to more purposefully explore Jesus' story. We learned that His life was filled with love, humility, courage, healing, battling demons, and performing miracles. At thirty-three years old, Jesus was betrayed, tortured, nailed to a cross, and He died a horrendous death. But that was not the end of Jesus' story. He overcame death and was resurrected back to life.

As we studied the life of Jesus, we found that an often-overlooked part of Jesus' story is that He longs to be part of each of our stories. You see, God took on human form to visit humankind—and He also visited us personally. We both remember the time in our lives when Jesus Christ, figuratively speaking, knocked on the door to our hearts.[5] In faith we said, "Yes, Lord!" We repented—turned away from sin—and invited Jesus into our hearts, lives, marriage, family—and stories. In fact, we asked Jesus to be the *main character* in our stories. Looking back over our lives, those are decisions neither one of us has ever regretted making.

As we studied the life of Jesus and reviewed recorded history, we could not find *one person* who impacted humankind more than Jesus Christ.

> **He was born in an obscure village, the child of a peasant woman. He worked in a carpentry shop until he was thirty, and then for three years he was an itinerant preacher. When the tide [of] popular opinion turned against him, his friends ran away. He was turned over to his enemies. He was tried and convicted. He was nailed upon a cross between two thieves. When he was dead, he was laid in a borrowed grave. He never wrote a book. He never held an office. He never owned a home. He never went to college. He never traveled more than two hundred miles from the place where he was born. He never did one of the things that usually accompanies greatness. Yet all the armies that ever marched, and all the governments that ever sat, and all the kings that ever reigned, [have] not affected life upon this earth as powerfully as that One Solitary Life.[6]**

✝ ✝ ✝

The Hope of the World

Throughout our travels, we meet men, women, and couples who believe traditional/orthodox marriage is dying and in need of CPR. But we are also meeting more and more people who are pushing back against the hijacked marriage narrative. And they are passionately embracing a marriage built on love, functional equality, mutuality, and reciprocal servanthood.

Looking to the future, we envision men and women—especially the emerging generations—humbly returning to God's creational marriage design. And as we continue to work with couples, we are truly hopeful about marriage. *Why?* Because our *hope* is based on the "living *hope* through the resurrection of Jesus Christ."[7]

We understand that many people are easily triggered and quickly become amped-up about the discussion, drama, and debate surrounding marriage. *Can everyone agree there is a lack of peace in our culture?* That said, we want to remind readers that true peace is not the absence of chaos or controversy—but the presence of love. *Love* is the essential ingredient in marriage, as well as in every relationship.

God is love,[8] and one essence of love includes *hope.* Our position is that it's *not* the church, religion, denominations, para-church organizations, pastors, politicians, pundits, political movements, pop-culture, partisan-tribalism, educational institutions, authors, activist bullies, elitism, celebrity personalities, twitter mobs, anonymous-keyboard cowards, identity politics, social media, or Supreme Court Justices who are the hope of the world.

We believe **JESUS CHRIST IS THE HOPE OF THE WORLD**.

+ + +

We Love Marriage!

After forty-three years of marriage, by God's grace—*and with lots of hard work*—we still say we *love being married.* And as we review walking out our calling to be *missionaries to marriage*, we are often asked, *Can you help us understand the motivation that has encouraged you for over four decades to invest your lives teaching and writing about God and marriage?*

That is a worthwhile question. As we invite God into our process (**I.O.T.L.**) and ponder our passion for God's creational marriage design, two specific things come to our hearts:

#1—EVERY PERSON MATTERS TO GOD—YOU MATTER TO GOD.
#2—GOD'S CREATIONAL MARRIAGE DESIGN MATTERS TO GOD.

At the beginning of this book, we asked readers to take an overview of their marriage. After completing this book, we want you to answer the same questions.

Date: _____

On a continuum from 1 to 10:

[1=Our marriage is very disconnected to 10=Our marriage couldn't be better]

How would you rate your marriage in this current season? _____

How do you think your spouse would rate your marriage in this current season? _____

As you consider your responses, make two observations related to your marriage in this current season. [Note: you will not be asked to share this.]

_____

_____

Concerning prayer, how would you rate your prayer life with your spouse? _____

How do you think your spouse would rate their prayer life with you? _____

As you consider your responses, make two observations specifically related to your prayer life. [Note: you will not be asked to share this.]

_____

_____

Throughout our REAL LIFE Marriage book series, we encourage couples to always have dreams for their marriage. And when you dream—dream BIG! Write down two marriage dreams you have in this season of your marriage.

_____

_____

APPENDIX A

THE TRAFFIC LIGHT PRINCIPLE

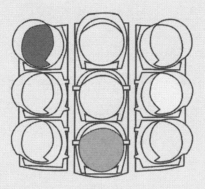

The **Traffic Light Principle** is about purposefully inviting God into your process. Implementing the **Traffic Light Principle** involves putting God first, trusting Him (Proverbs 3:5–6), and asking for wisdom (James 1:5). Our real life experience has taught us that purposefully including God in our decision-making process provides us with power, protection, and opportunities to advance in intimacy and experience more frequent SOULgasms.

How Does the Traffic Light Principle Work?

Step 1: A husband and wife individually **I.O.T.L.** (*Inquire of the Lord*). They invite God into their decision-making process and seek His wisdom. The Bible says, "If any of you lacks wisdom, you should ask God, who gives generously to all without finding fault, and it will be given to you" (James 1:5 NIV).

Step 2: The second step involves couples sharing what they sense the Lord may be saying. Figuratively speaking, are they sensing a "green light" (*go*); a "yellow light" (*slow*); or a "red light" (*no*)?

Step 3: Couples wait until they both have "green lights" from God; then they pull the trigger on the decision.

In addition, we encourage couples to agree on the following principles:

1. Proceed only if you are in unity. If you do not both have "green lights" from the Lord, agree to wait because unity with God and each other should trump disunity.

2. If your lights remain different while you are waiting, continue to pray—and listen. The Bible says, "See to it that you do not refuse Him who is speaking" (Hebrews 12:25). If appropriate, include a third party for insight and wisdom. "Where there is no guidance the people fall, But in abundance of counselors there is victory" (Proverbs 11:14). Keep revisiting your decision until you sense God giving you both "green lights."

3. As you continue to process, it is important to understand the key component in the **Traffic Light Principle**: It includes three lights. The middle light represents God, one light represents what the wife senses from God, and one light represents what the husband senses from God.

Following are questions couples often ask about the **Traffic Light Principle**:

+ *Is a couple's main goal to be in agreement?*

No, remember Adam and Eve were in agreement when they ate the forbidden fruit—and we all know how that played out. Had either Eve or Adam asked God for a light, it would have been bright red. Therefore, a couple's agreement must be based on what they *both* sense the Lord saying.

+ *With all the time it takes to implement the* Traffic Light Principle, *taking time necessary to I.O.T.L. and to pray and process, how do you ever get around to making decisions?*

Early in our marriage, one of us would try to "work it" to get what they wanted, even if we did not have unity. This resulted in the decision often ending in a disaster. Implementing the **Traffic Light Principle**, even if it means slowing your decision-making process down, encourages couples to include God.

+ Do you use the Traffic Light Principle on every decision?

That is a good question. For example, we do not call our spouse from the grocery store and ask, "Do you have a green light on Granny Smith or Honeycrisp apples?" God created men and women as volitional human beings who have been given the ability to make choices. Therefore, couples can choose to include God on decisions or not—the choice is up to them.

The Bible says, "You do not have because you do not ask" (James 4:2). It also says, "If you want favor with both God and man, and a reputation for good judgment and common sense, then trust the Lord completely; don't ever trust yourself. In *everything* you do, put God first, and *he will direct you* and crown your efforts with success" (Proverbs 3:4-6 TLB). The bottom line is, couples don't *have* to include God and walk *together* in unity—they *get* to.

+ Marriage has so much untapped, kingdom-advancing potential. Why?

There is power and protection in covenant—in "two becoming one" (Genesis 2:24). Walking in unity opens the door for couples to fully celebrate what it means to be "naked without shame" (Genesis 2:25). Furthermore, living out God's creational marriage design—as co-leaders, functional equals, and reciprocal servants—provides amazing opportunities to share with others about GOD—the Maker of marriage.

Having lived out the **Traffic Light Principle** for decades, there is one essential ingredient we've found to successfully implementing it. **This principle presupposes the husband and wife have a measure of emotional health, humility, and tender-teachable hearts.** If either spouse is controlling, demanding, discounting, or disrespectful toward their spouse, it will minimize the couple's ability to experience success in this unity principle. For example, after a teaching about the **Traffic Light Principle**, one husband said, "So, if I tell my wife I have a yellow or red light, then she can't do what she wants—right?"

Sadly, this husband missed the entire point of this principle. After engaging with him, it became apparent that he never included God, and his red or yellow light was a way to attempt to gain control, get his own way, or keep his wife from doing something she sensed the Lord saying. If either spouse defaults to immaturity, control, disunity, or disagreement and lives in the smaller story where *self* is the main character (instead of living in the Larger Story where *God* is the main character), the blessings this principle provides will be derailed. That said, if a couple reaches a logjam, we strongly encourage them to invite a mature third party to help process making decisions.

We've experienced the blessings and benefits of including God and making decisions when we *both* have green lights from the Lord. And we would never revert to one of us having the final say, to Tim—as the husband—having a gender trump card, or to basing our decisions solely on individual gifts.

As we look back over four decades of marriage, implementing the **Traffic Light Principle** has resulted in increased intimacy with God and each other as *together* we've *advanced* in intimacy and spirit + soul + body oneness.

APPENDIX B

LISTENING TO GOD

Listening to God is one of the most important things a Christ-follower can do. The Bible says, "See to it that you do not refuse Him who is speaking" (Hebrews 12:25). Following are questions that are listed in our book *TOGETHER: Reclaiming Co-Leadership in Marriage* to help a person's (and couple's) decision-making process:

1. Have you prayed about what you are considering?

"Be anxious for nothing, but in everything by prayer and supplication with thanksgiving let your requests be known to God" (Philippians 4:6).

"Take every thought captive to obey Christ" (2 Corinthians 10:5 ESV).

2. Is what you are considering consistent with the principles in the Bible?

"He who is spiritual appraises all things" (1 Corinthians 2:15).

"If any of you lacks wisdom, let him ask of God, who gives to all generously and without reproach" (James 1:5).

3. Is what you are considering affirmed by other godly people?

"Where there is no guidance [revelation] the people fall, But in abundance of counselors there is victory" (Proverbs 11:14).

4. Will what you are considering bring glory to God?

"Whatever you do in word and deed, do all in the name of the Lord Jesus" (Colossians 3:17).

5. Will what you are considering positively impact God's kingdom?

"Seek first His kingdom and His righteousness" (Matthew 6:33).

Remember, the kingdom of God has one King (and the King is not the husband).

6. How does what you are considering relate to God's will for your life?

"Rejoice always; pray without ceasing; in everything give thanks; for this is God's will for you in Christ Jesus" (1 Thessalonians 5:16-18).

7. Do you have peace about what you are considering?

"And the peace of God, which surpasses all understanding, will guard your hearts and your minds in Christ Jesus" (Philippians 4:7 ESV).

8. Do you have unity with your spouse?

God's creational design for marriage included mutuality, shared leadership, and functional authority—what we call co-leadership (Genesis 1 and 2).

9. Will what you are considering cost you something?

"And He said to them, 'Truly I say to you, there is no one who has left house or wife or brothers or parents or children, for the sake of the kingdom of God, who will not receive many times as much at this time and in the age to come, eternal life" (Luke 18:29-30). Remember—cost is not always money; it often involves servanthood, sacrifice, humility, and taking the road less traveled.

10. Does what you are considering agree with your life calling and mission?

"I therefore ... urge you to walk in a manner worthy of the calling to which you have been called" (Ephesians 4:1 ESV).

"Who has saved us and called us with a holy calling, not according to our works, but according to His own purpose and grace which was granted us in Christ Jesus" (2 Timothy 1:9).

11. Does what you are considering come from a pure heart?

"The Lord does not look at the things people look at. People look at the outward appearance, but the Lord looks at the heart" (1 Samuel 16:7 NLT).

"The mouth speaks out of that which fills the heart" (Matthew 12:34).

12. Does what you are considering come from a place of love?

"You shall love the Lord your God with all your heart, and with all your soul, and with all your mind." This is the great and foremost commandment. The second is like it, "You shall love your neighbor as yourself." On these two commandments depend the whole Law and the Prophets" (Matthew 22:37-40).

The older we get, the more we believe that *love is the ball game!* The most mature followers of Christ we have known throughout our lives have been the most loving people we know.

This non-exhaustive list is not based on gender. Notice that each step equally impacts both men and women. Again, in marriage, three keys to co-leading together and making godly decisions are:

    1. **I.O.T.L.** (*Inquire of the Lord*)

    2. Maximize both the wife's and husband's gifts.

    3. Implement the **Traffic Light Principle** and wait for unity (until you both have "green lights" from the Lord).

APPENDIX C

I.O.T.L.—INQUIRE OF THE LORD

I.O.T.L. is a simple four-letter acronym that stands for "Inquire of the Lord."

I.O.T.L. is about seeking the presence of God. In the New Testament, the apostle Paul emphasized the importance of "taking every thought captive to the obedience of Christ" (2 Corinthians 10:5 NIV).

And throughout the Old Testament, when leaders "inquired of the Lord," they experienced victories (Judges 20:23; Judges 20:27; 1 Samuel 23:2,4; 2 Samuel 5:23; 1 Chronicles 14:10).

If you are a follower of Jesus Christ, the Holy Spirit dwells in you (1 Corinthians 6:19; Romans 8:9; 1 Corinthians 3:16).

Therefore, it is wise to "take captive every thought to make it obedient to Christ" (2 Corinthians 10:5 NIV) and include Him in everything. Including God provides power and protection.

> **+ I.O.T.L.** is a reminder to invite God into your life, your marriage, and the decisions you make.

> **+ I.O.T.L.** includes putting God first, trusting Him (Proverbs 3:5–6), and asking for wisdom (James 1:5).

> **+ I.O.T.L.** will provide you with insight that no authors, teachers, or pastors/priests can provide.

Remember, **I.O.T.L.** is *not* a religious exercise. It involves a person relating to God. Picture a child saying to a good mommy/daddy, "I trust you. Please give me wisdom and help me to make good decisions." Similar to co-leading together, **I.O.T.L.** and including God in our decision-making process is not something we *have* to do; instead it's something we *get* to do.

ACKNOWLEDGMENTS

Life is lived in a story … and writing this book has been a story filled with family and friends. Our experience is that anything successful in life involves a team. God built an amazing team for this project. The reality is there are too many team members to list. Nevertheless, we want to extend our heartfelt thanks to the following people:

+ To our Prayer Shield Team who pray for us, our marriage, family, ministry, teaching, writing, and *missionaries to marriage* calling. We treasure your prayers and encouragement.

+ To our parents, Bill and Jeanne Evans and Jack and Pat O'Shaughnessy, for laying a strong foundation that continues to be built on.

+ To our children: Tim, Amy and Curt, Colleen and Johnny, and Cate and Darren. Thank you for being willing to follow God—even when it cost you something. And to our grandchildren: Joel, Trey, Grace, Emma, Jack, Jay … and future grandkids (& great-grandkids). Your existence brings us indescribable joy!

+ To our amazing REAL LIFE friends and partners: Jim and Kathy Kubik, Keith and Robyn Brodie, TJ and Deb Bratt, George and Melodee Cook, Adam and Jill Carter, Laurence and Jessica Coppedge, David and Kate Kubik, Daniel and Jackie Hathaway, Jason and Keeley Cormier, Bill and Barb Vroon, Chuck and Bev Osterink, Jennifer and Ben Slenk, Tom and Julie Vroon, Doug and Nicole LaCroix, Danny and Angela Gieck, Paul and Barb Osburn, Kate and Troy DeWys, Justin Ensor, and many others. Our gratitude for your ongoing prayers, partnership, and belief in us is difficult to put into words—*thank you*.

+ To: Amy Calkins for editing; Michael Murdock for interior layout and text pour in; Beryl Glass for our cover design and illustration; and Amy DeBoer for the picture. You all became key partners in the completion of this project.

+ While writing this book, we were blessed to be on the receiving end of encouraging words and timely support that cheered us on. To Ken Gire and Brad Herman for your ongoing encouragement to keep writing. Special thanks to: Linda Laird, Jack and Becky Sytsema, Mary and Mike Banas, Jodi and Miles Anderson, Stephanie and Jay Frankhouse, Zach and Jordyn Osburn, John Tekautz, Tom and Jan Murray, Marty and Marilyn O'Connor, Chester and Betsy Kylstra, Doris (Peter) Wagner, and Gilbert Bilezikian, Dan and Jane Evans, Anne and Mike Risher, John and Caryl O'Shaughnessy, Jack and Terri Brown, Donna and Terry Simale, Jae and Alissa Edwards, Traci and Travis Hearns, John and Kem Stickl, Scott and Melissa Motschenbacher, Cindi and Lee Whitman, and Jacob and Hannah Oulette. Mike Ruman, Michelle Dabeq, Charles Cash, Tom Stella ... and so many others. Thank you for your prayers, notes, calls, feedback, and gestures of kindness that arrived at the perfect times.

+ A special thank you to those who are represented (anonymously) through the stories in this book; and to the men and women in our co-leadership marriage community groups through-out the decades. Your lives tell stories that points us to God. Thank you for having the cour-age to share the joys and struggles of your journey. Seeing you advance in intimacy with God and each other inspires us to keep trusting God—and taking risks.

+ We thank God for and we bless others who will build on what we have written about God's creational marriage design and co-leadership in marriage. Our prayer is that God builds a network of relationships united in heart about a marriage mission that matters.

+ Lastly, we thank God for creating marriage. It's our prayer that Your creational marriage design is passionately reclaimed and humbly restored.

ABOUT THE AUTHORS

Photo by Amy DeBoer.

Tim+Anne Evans love marriage! They have been married forty-three years and have coun-seled couples for decades. They are both ordained ministers, and each has master and doctor of practical ministry diplomas from Wagner Leadership Institute. They are parents, grandparents, pastoral counselors, authors, and marriage mentors. Tim is a retired fire chief. Anne is a licensed nurse and certified life-purpose coach. They live in Colorado Springs, co-lead REAL LIFE Ministries, and *together* walk out their calling as *missionaries to marriage*.

REAL LIFE MINISTRIES

REAL LIFE Ministries' mission is to help men, women, and couples advance in passionately loving God, loving a spouse, and loving others (Matthew 22:37-40). The *why* that drives REAL LIFE is Marriage Transformation.

REAL LIFE offers:

+ Pastoral counseling

+ Marriage tune-ups

+ Marriage intensives

+ REAL LIFE Marriage Advance weekend seminars

+ TOGETHER: Reclaiming Co-Leadership in Marriage workshop

+ NAKED: Reclaiming Sexual Intimacy in Marriage workshop

+ SOULgasm: Caring for Your Soul and the Soul of Your Marriage workshop

+ COMMUNICATION: A Key to Advancing in Intimacy workshop

+ PRAYER: Talking with God workshop

+ FORGIVENESS: Begins with a Decision workshop

+ Seven Keys to Advancing in Intimacy with Your Spouse workshop

+ Premarital counseling

+ Men's and women's gatherings

tim+anne evans

REAL LIFE ministries

www.TimPlusAnne.com

PO Box 6800 Colorado Springs, CO 80934

NOTES

Notes to Readers

1. Tim and Anne Evans, *TOGETHER: Reclaiming Co-Leadership in Marriage* (Colorado Springs, CO: REAL LIFE Ministries, 2014). Available at Amazon.com.
2. Tim and Anne Evans, *NAKED: Reclaiming Sexual Intimacy in Marriage* (Colorado Springs, CO: REAL LIFE Ministries, 2017). Available at Amazon.com.
3. Tim and Anne Evans, *SOULgasm: Caring for Your Soul and the Soul of Your Marriage* (Colorado Springs, CO: REAL LIFE Ministries, 2018). Available at Amazon.com.
4. Tim and Anne Evans, *COMMUNICATION: A Key to Advancing in Intimacy* (Colorado Springs, CO: REAL LIFE Ministries, 2020). Available at Amazon.com.
5. James Emery White, "Meet Generation ... Alpha," *CHURCH & CULTURE* blog (January 24, 2019); www.churchandculture.org/blog/2019/1/24/meet-generation-alpha (accessed July 7, 2019).

Preface: LIFE IS LIVED IN A STORY

1. Colossians 4:2
2. We first heard about the concept of Larger Story vs. smaller story from the teachings and writings of Dr. Dan B. Allender and John Eldredge.
3. Proverbs 29:18 KJV

Chapter 1: THE MYSTERY OF PRAYER

1. Richard J. Foster, *Prayer: Finding the Heart's True Home* (New York: HarperCollins, 1992), as quoted on the dustjacket.
2. Genesis 2:24
3. James 1:5
4. Hebrews 12:25
5. Philippians 4:6
6. James 1:5
7. Phillip Yancey, *Prayer: Does It Make Any Difference?* (Grand Rapids, MI: Zondervan, 2010), 191–192.
8. Genesis 2:24
9. Genesis 2:25
10. Hebrews 12:25
11. James 1:5
12. Luke 11:1b
13. Luke 11:1

14. We first heard the phrase *ordinary and extraordinary* moments in the movie *About Time*.
15. Luke 11:2
16. Leviticus 19:2
17. Genesis 1:27
18. 2 Corinthians 13:14
19. Genesis 2:24
20. Hebrews 12:25
21. Deuteronomy 6:5–9
22. 1 Corinthians 13:11
23. Proverbs 34:8

Chapter 2: LISTENING TO GOD

1. Our book, *COMMUNICATION: A Key to Advancing in Intimacy*, unpacks communicating and listening well.
2. Mother Theresa, quoted on www.goodreads.com/quotes/252954-in-the-silence-of-the-heart-god-speaks-if-you.
3. Hebrews 12:25 NIV
4. Hebrews 12:25 NLT
5. Romans 1:20
6. Our favorite poet is John Blase—*the beautiful due*—https://johnblase.com.
7. 1 Kings 19:12b
8. 2 Chronicles 16:9 NIV
9. Hebrews 12:25

Chapter 3: WORDS HAVE POWER

1. Socrates, "Essential Thinkers—Socrates," quoted on www.goodreads.com/quotes/823818-is-it-true-is-it-kind-or-is-it-necessary (accessed Feb 12, 2020).
2. Proverbs 18:21 NIV
3. Matthew 12:34
4. Genesis 1:3
5. Genesis 1:6
6. Genesis 1:9
7. Genesis 1:11
8. Genesis 1:14–15
9. Genesis 1:20
10. Genesis 1:24
11. Genesis 1:28
12. Genesis 2:18
13. Genesis 1:27
14. The *Forgiveness Model* is explained in chapter 5 of our forthcoming book, *FORGIVENESS: A Key to Advancing in Intimacy*.

Chapter 4: WHO + WHAT + WHEN + WHY + WHERE OF PRAYER

1. 1 Thessalonians 5:17
2. Philippians 4:6a
3. James 1:5
4. Matthew 26:39; Luke 23:34
5. Luke 11:1–4
6. John 11:41
7. Luke 18:1
8. Philippians 4:4–7
9. Parker Palmer, quoted on, https://onbeing.org/blog/seeking-sanctuary-in-our-own-sacred-spaces.

Chapter 5: PRAYING WITHOUT CEASING

1. 2 Corinthians 13:5 NIV
2. We first heard this phrase in a sermon preached by Colleen Evans Stickl at Valley Creek Church, Flower Mound, Texas on Mother's Day, May 12, 2019; http://www.ValleyCreek.org.
3. 2 Corinthians 13:5 NIV
4. 1 Peter 5:5b
5. 1 Thessalonians 5:17
6. 1 Thessalonians 5:17

Chapter 6: PRAYING INCREASES INTIMACY

1. 2 Corinthians 10:5 NIV
2. Hebrews 12:25 NLT

Chapter 7: PRAYER AND GOD'S WILL

1. 1 Thessalonians 5:16–18
2. Luke 18:1–8 NIV

Chapter 8: LIST PRAYING

1. Colossians 4:2
2. 1 Timothy 2:1–4 NLT
3. Max Lucado, quoted on www.goodreads.com/quotes/813471-our-prayers-may-be-awkward-our-attempts-may-be-feeble.
4. James 5:16 MSG
5. James 5:16 MSG

Chapter 9: PRAYING SCRIPTURE

1. Romans 12:1
2. Ephesians 6:10-17 NIV
3. Philippians 4:4-7 NIV
4. Psalm 119:11

Chapter 10: PRAYER AND SPIRITUAL WARFARE

1. James 1:2-4
2. 1 Corinthians 7:28b
3. James 1:3
4. Matthew 13:39; Luke 10:18; 11:18
5. Ezekiel 28:14
6. Ephesians 6:11-12
7. Ezekiel 28:14
8. Ezekiel 28:12
9. John 8:44
10. John 8:44
11. 1 John 3:8
12. Revelation 12:10
13. 1 Peter 5:8
14. Luke 4:10-11
15. John 10:10
16. Matthew 22:37-40
17. Matthew 4:1-11
18. Matthew 6:13
19. Proverbs 4:23
20. 1 Corinthians 16:10 NIV
21. 1 John 4:18a NIV
22. 1 John 4:4 NIV
23. Ephesians 6:12
24. John 10:10a
25. John 10:10b
26. Proverbs 11:14

Chapter 11: STRATEGIC PRAYER

1. Psalm 37:4 NIV
2. James 4:2b NIV
3. Matthew 6:5-7 NIV
4. Matthew 6:8 NIV
5. Romans 8:26 MSG
6. Galatians 5:22
7. Philippians 4:7
8. This prayer is adapted from the teachings of Dr. Chester and Betsy Kylstra, Restoring the Foundations ministry, www.restoringthefoundations.org.

9.   We received this prayer from Gary and Danice Duda, Restoring the Foundations trainers and ministers.
10. Genesis 3:1 NIV
11. Romans 8:9
12   Romans 12:1
13. A good book regarding food addiction is: *Breaking the Stronghold of Food: How We Conquered Food Addictions and Discovered a New Way of Living*, by Michael L. Brown with Nancy Brown (Lake Mary, FL: Siloam Charisma Media/Charisma House Book Group, 2017).
14. Much of this list is taken from www.addictioncenter.com/addiction/10-most-common-addictions.
15. In our book, *SOULgasm*, Chapter 12 describes how choosing pride over humility is a SOUL-gasm-blocker.
16. James 4:6
17. Matthew 23:12
18. 1 Peter 5:5
19. Numbers 20:8–11
20. Genesis 1:26–28
21. John Eldredge, *Ransomed Heart Newsletter* (Sept/Oct 2019).
22. Galatians 5:22
23. Rory Nolan, "Holy Spirit Take Control," www.willowcreek.com/docs/willowcharts/samples/633277103909_HolySpiritTakeControl_OBASIC_sample.PDF.
24. James 4:2b NIV

Chapter 12: DEVELOPING A PRAYER SHIELD

1.   C. Peter Wagner, Prayer Shield, The Prayer Warrior Series (Ventura, CA: Regal, 1992).
2.   Matthew 7:7
3.   Mother Theresa, quoted at www.azquotes.com/quote/535083.

Chapter 13: THE PRACTICE OF SURRENDER

1.   Psalm 46:10

Chapter 14: HUSBANDS ARE YOUR PRAYERS HINDERED?

1.   1 Peter 3:7
2.   1 Peter 2:21,23
3.   *Oxford Dictionary*.
4.   1 Peter 3:7
5.   1 Peter 3:4
6.   1 Peter 3:7
7.   1 Peter 3:7a
8.   1 Peter 3:7
9.   Ephesians 5:21 NIV
10. We explain our beliefs about biblical headship in our book *TOGETHER Reclaiming Co-Leadershipin Marriage*.
11. 1 Corinthians 7:4
12. 1 Peter 3:7

13. *Oxford Dictionary*.
14. 1 Peter 3:7
15. Ephesians 5:21
16. Genesis 3:16
17. Luke 11:1
18. 1 Peter 3:8–9 NIV

Chapter 15: PRAYING TOGETHER

1. Ecclesiastes 4:9 NIV
2. Thomas Merton, *Conjectures of a Guilty Bystander* (New York: Image Classic, 1968; reprint 2009), 72.
3. Matthew 18:19–20 NLT
4. 1 John 4:4
5. Psalm 46:10

Chapter 16: LEAVING A PRAYER LEGACY

1. 1 Samuel 13:14
2. Ezekiel 22:30
3. Colossians 4:2
4. James 5:16b NIV
5. 2 Chronicles 7:14 NKJV
6. Deuteronomy 32:30a
7. Genesis 2:24
8. Ephesians 6:10–18
9. 1 Peter 5:5
10. 1 John 4:4
11. Genesis 2:24

Chapter 17: 25 THINGS THAT CAN HINDER PRAYERS

1. James 4:2 NIV
2. Matthew 7:7-8 NIV
3. Frederick Buechner, "Prayer," April 4, 2016; www.frederickbuechner.com/quote-of-the-day/2016/4/25/prayer (accessed Feb. 26, 2020).
4. James 4:3 TPT
5. Philippians 2:3-4 NIV
6. James 4:6
7. Mark 11:25 NIV
8. We are putting the finishing touches on our upcoming book, *FORGIVENESS: Begins With a Decision*, available soon.
9. James 1:5-7
10. Matthew 21:22 ESV
11. Matthew 21:22
12. Proverbs 3:5-8 TPT
13. John Eldredge, *Get Your Life Back Today* (Nashville, TN: Thomas Nelson, 2020), 158–159.
14. 1 John 4:18 NIV

15. We first learned about godly and ungodly beliefs in Restoring the Foundations training led by Dr. Chester and Betsy Kylstra, www.restoringthefoundations.org, Hendersonville, North Carolina.
16. Isaiah 59:2 NKJV
17. Psalm 55:18 NKJV
18. Isaiah 59:2
19. Isaiah 59:1–2
20. Psalm 66:18 NLT
21. Frederick Buechner, *Telling Secrets* (New York: HarperOne, 2009).
22. Psalm 84:11 NIV
23. Exodus 20:12 ESB
24. Galatians 6:7
25. Mother Theresa, quoted at www.brainyquote.com/quotes/mother_teresa_164357.
26. Queen, "I Want It All," *The Miracle Album* (1989), sung by Freddy Mercury.
27. Ryan Holiday, quoted at www.brainyquote.com/topics/perfectionism-quotes.
28. Brene Brown, quoted at www.brainyquote.com/topics/perfectionism-quotes.
29. Frederick Buechner, "Prayer," April 4, 2016; www.frederickbuechner.com/quote-of-the-day/2016/4/25/prayer (accessed Feb. 26, 2020).
30. Colleen Evans Stickl, "Mother's Day message 2019," Valley Creek Church, www.ValleyCreek.org.
31. 1 Peter 3:7
32. Deuteronomy 32:30 TLB
33. Parker Palmer, *Let Your Life Speak: Listening for the Voice of Vocation*, quoted on www.goodreads.com/quotes/1335101-self-care-is-never-a-selfish-act---it-is-simply.
34. Paul Byerly, "Daily Generous Husband Daily Rants on Being a Better Husband," *The Generous Husband* (Feb 23, 2020); www.the-generous-husband.com/2020/02/23/self-care-vs-self-soothing.
35. Proverbs 4:23
36. Matthew 12:34
37. Philippians 4:4–8 NIV
38. Ephesians 6:12 NIV
39. Ephesians 6:18–20 NIV
40. Oswald Chambers, quoted at www.goodreads.com/author/quotes/41469.Oswald_Chambers.
41. Proverbs 3:5–6
42. Matthew 22:36–40 NIV
43. 1 Corinthians 13:8 NIV
44. 1 Corinthians 13:13 NIV
45. Colossians 4:2 NIV
46. John 15:4
47. Isaiah 59:2 NKJV
48. Isaiah 59:2

Chapter 18: WHAT IF MY PRAYERS ARE NOT ANSWERED IN THE WAY I WANT?

1. Matthew 21:22 NIV
2. Oswald Chambers, quoted on https://quotefancy.com/quote/883233/Oswald-Chambers-Our-Lord-never-referred-to-unanswered-prayer-he-taught-that-prayers-are.
3. Anne Lamont, quoted on www.relicsworld.com/anne-lamott/ive-seen-prayers-answered-but-often-in-my-experiences-if-you-author-anne-lamott.
4. Jim George, quoted on www.quotes.wiki/when-your-prayers-arent-answered-immediately.

5. Lloyd John Ogilvie, quoted on *https://quotefancy.com/quote/1598041/Lloyd-John-Ogilvie-All-prayers-are-answered-We-need-to-distinguish-between-a-prayer*.
6. Mother Theresa, quoted on https://spiritualbridge.org/walking-in-gods-ways/christian-parenting/mother-teresa-prayer-is-not-asking-prayer-is-putting-oneself-in-the-hands-of-god-at-his-disposition-and-listening-to-his-voice-in-the-depth-of-our-hearts/#.Xmb1CkBFxKo.
7. C.S. Lewis, *God In The Dock*; quoted on https://redeeminggod.com/work-and-prayer-by-c-s-lewis.
8. 1 John 5:14
9. Mark 11:24
10. Matthew 7:7
11. Matthew 21:22
12. Isaiah 55:8–9
13. 2 Corinthians 12:8–9 NIV
14. We unpack this throughout our book *TOGETHER Reclaiming Co-Leadership in Marriage* (2014).
15. Genesis 1:28a NIV
16. Genesis 1:28b NIV
17. Genesis 1:26
18. Genesis 3:8a
19. Genesis 2:25
20. Genesis 2:27
21. Genesis 3:1
22. Genesis 3:16
23. Galatians 4:4–7
24. John 16:17
25. James 1:2–3 NIV
26. Isaiah 55:8–9
27. Matthew 28:20
28. Hebrews 13:5 NIV
29. Author unknown. Often the credit is given to Mary Stevenson, Margaret Fishback Powers, or Carolyn Joyce Carty, who have all registered copyrights for the poem.
30. 1 Corinthians 13:12 NIV
31. Garth Brooks, quoted on www.goodreads.com/quotes/225489-some-of-god-s-greatest-gifts-are-unanswered-prayers.
32. Deuteronomy 29:29a NIV

Chapter 19: NEXT STEPS

1. Appendix C
2. Appendix A
3. Matthew 22:37–40
4. 1 Corinthians 7:28b

Epilogue: MARRIAGE IS NOT "IT"

1. 1 Corinthians 7:28b
2. Genesis 2:24
3. Genesis 2:25

4. God's creational marriage design is addressed in our book *TOGETHER: Reclaiming Co-Leadership in Marriage* (Colorado Springs, CO: REAL LIFE Ministries, 2014). Available at Amazon.com.
5. Revelation 3:20
6. Author unknown.
7. 1 Peter 1:3 NIV
8. 1 John 4:16

REAL LIFE BOOKS

TOGETHER
Reclaiming **Co-Leadership** in Marriage

tim+anne evans

TOGETHER
COMPANION JOURNAL

Reclaiming **Co-Leadership** in Marriage

anne+tim evans

Includes Facilitator's Guide

NAKED
Reclaiming **Sexual Intimacy** in Marriage

tim+anne evans

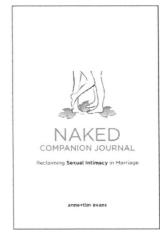

NAKED
COMPANION JOURNAL

Reclaiming **Sexual Intimacy** in Marriage

anne+tim evans

SOULgasm
Caring for Your **Soul** and the **Soul** of Your Marriage

tim+anne evans

SOULgasm
COMPANION JOURNAL

Caring for Your **Soul** and the **Soul** of Your Marriage

anne+tim evans

Available on Amazon.com

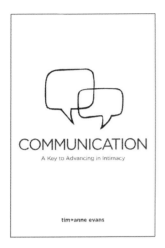

COMMUNICATION

A Key to Advancing in Intimacy

tim+anne evans

PRAYER

Talking with God

tim+anne evans

Coming Soon

FORGIVENESS

Begins With a Decision

tim+anne evans

ABUSE

Experiencing Freedom Through Forgiveness

tim+anne evans

PRAYER

Talking with God

May the God who is both great and good
make your marriage stronger and your hearts braver.
May He create not only a willingness to die for your marriage,
but also a passion to live for it.

Made in the USA
San Bernardino, CA
02 July 2020

74632525R00149